Broccoli Cookbook

A Vegatable Cookbook Filled with Delicious Broccoli Recipes

By
BookSumo Press

Published by
http://www.booksumo.com

ENJOY THE RECIPES?

KEEP ON COOKING
WITH 6 MORE FREE COOKBOOKS!

Visit our website and simply enter your email address to join the club and receive your 6 cookbooks.

http://booksumo.com/magnet

https://www.instagram.com/booksumopress/

https://www.facebook.com/booksumo/

LEGAL NOTES

Table of Contents

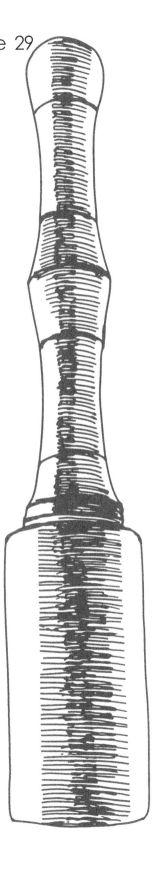

Cream of Cauliflower Bake 71

Cauliflower Salad I 72

Beef & Broccoli 73

Broccoli Pepper Cheddar Grilled Cheese 74

Garden Lasagna I 75

Pepperoni Rotini Pasta Salad 76

Linguine Romano Pasta Salad 77

Ravioli & Broccoli Pasta Salad 78

Mac and Cheese Soup 79

Cheesy Onion and Potato Soup 80

Cream of Mushrooms and Broccoli 81

2 Cheese Chicken Casserole 82

Swiss Style Broccoli Casserole 83

Sweet Potato Wraps 84

A Quiche of Lentils and Cheese 86

Swiss Style Broccoli Casserole 87

Classic Chicken and Rice 88

Broccoli and Cheddar Quinoa 90

Southeast Asian Tofu with Broccoli 91

Thai Stir-Fry Noodle 92

Red Pepper Broccoli 93

Broccoli
Sunflower Salad

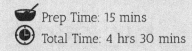 Prep Time: 15 mins

Total Time: 4 hrs 30 mins

Servings per Recipe: 6

Calories	559 kcal
Fat	48.1 g
Carbohydrates	23.9 g
Protein	12.9 g
Cholesterol	31 mg
Sodium	584 mg

Ingredients

10 slices bacon
1 head fresh broccoli, cut into bite size pieces
1/4 C. red onion, diced
1/2 C. raisins
3 tbsps white wine vinegar
2 tbsps white sugar

1 C. mayonnaise
1 C. sunflower seeds

Directions

1. Stir fry your bacon until crispy then break it into pieces.
2. Get a bowl, combine: raisins, broccoli, and onions.
3. Get a 2nd bowl, combine: mayo, sugar, and vinegar.
4. Combine both bowls then place a covering of plastic around the bowl.
5. Put everything in the fridge for 4 hours.
6. Add in your bacon and stir the salad. Then add the sunflower seeds as a topping.
7. Enjoy.

GRILLED
Chicken Salad

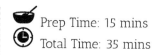
Prep Time: 15 mins
Total Time: 35 mins

Servings per Recipe: 6

Calories	239 kcal
Fat	11.1 g
Carbohydrates	17.5g
Protein	17.2 g
Cholesterol	43 mg
Sodium	69 mg

Ingredients

1/2 C. orange juice
1/2 C. white wine vinegar
1/4 C. olive oil
4 tbsps salt-free garlic and herb seasoning blend
1 1/2 tbsps white sugar
1 lb skinless, boneless chicken breast halves

1 head romaine lettuce- rinsed, dried and diced
1 (11 oz.) can mandarin oranges, drained
1 C. diced fresh broccoli
1 C. diced baby carrots

Directions

1. Get your grill hot and oil the grate.
2. Get a bowl, combine: sugar, orange juice, seasoning blend, olive oil, and vinegar.
3. Reserve half of a C. of this mix for later.
4. Cook your chicken for 7 mins, each side, on the grill, and coat the meat with the reserved mix often.
5. Get a 2nd bowl, combine: carrots, lettuce, broccoli, and oranges.
6. Julienne your chicken after it has been cooked then add it in with the orange mix and pour in the dressing.
7. Enjoy.

Cheesy
Veggie Quinoa

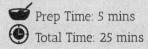 Prep Time: 5 mins

Total Time: 25 mins

Servings per Recipe: 4	
Calories	299 kcal
Fat	12.3 g
Carbohydrates	32.9 g
Protein	14.8 g
Cholesterol	30 mg
Sodium	491 mg

Ingredients

2 C. chopped broccoli
1 3/4 C. vegetable broth
1 C. quinoa

1 C. shredded Cheddar cheese
salt and ground black pepper to taste

Directions

1. Boil, in a big pot: quinoa, broccoli, and broth.
2. Once boiling place a lid on the pot and lower the heat.
3. Let the quinoa gently boil for 17 mins. Then add your cheese.
4. Cook everything for 4 more mins until the cheese is melted and then add your preferred amount of pepper and salt.
5. Enjoy.

TARA'S
Favorite Quinoa

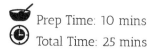
Prep Time: 10 mins
Total Time: 25 mins

Servings per Recipe: 4
Calories	264 kcal
Fat	12.3 g
Carbohydrates	31.9 g
Protein	7.1 g
Cholesterol	0 mg
Sodium	248 mg

Ingredients

1/2 C. uncooked quinoa
1 C. water
1 (15 oz.) can garbanzo beans, drained
3/4 C. chopped broccoli
1 clove garlic, minced, or to taste
1 tbsp fresh lemon juice
1 tsp dried tarragon
2 tsps coarse-grain mustard

3 tbsps extra virgin olive oil
salt and black pepper to taste

Directions

1. Boil your quinoa in water, lower the heat, place a lid on the pot, and cook for 17 mins.
2. Add everything to a bowl with: olive oil, beans, mustard, broccoli, tarragon, lemon, and garlic.
3. Enjoy warm or chilled after adding your preferred amount of pepper and salt.

Cream of Quinoa Casserole

Prep Time: 10 mins
Total Time: 1 hr 20 mins

Servings per Recipe: 6
Calories	494 kcal
Fat	32.1 g
Carbohydrates	39.8g
Protein	10.3 g
Cholesterol	31 mg
Sodium	1003 mg

Ingredients

1 C. quinoa
2 C. water
1 tsp olive oil
1 tsp salt
2 C. chopped broccoli
1 (10 oz.) can low-sodium cream of mushroom soup

1 C. shredded Cheddar cheese
1/2 C. French-fried onions
1/2 C. light sour cream
1 tsp lemon pepper
salt and ground black pepper to taste
1/2 C. French-fried onions

Directions

1. For 35 mins let your quinoa sit submerged in water.
2. Then use a strainer to rinse the quinoa under cold water before boiling it in fresh water and 1 tsp of salt and olive oil.
3. Once boiling place a lid on the pot, lower the heat, and let it cook for 22 mins.
4. Set your oven to 350 degrees before doing anything else.
5. For 7 mins steam your broccoli over 2 inches of boiling water with a steamer insert and a big pot.
6. Now add the following to your quinoa: lemon pepper, broccoli, sour cream, soup, fried onions, and cheese.
7. Top everything with some pepper and salt and stir everything.
8. Add everything to a casserole dish and cook it all in the oven for 15 mins.
9. Enjoy.

CREAM
of Frittata

Prep Time: 15 mins
Total Time: 40 mins

Servings per Recipe: 6
Calories   220.4 kcal
Cholesterol   199.5mg
Sodium   693.1mg
Carbohydrates   5.7g
Protein   12.3g

Ingredients

4 tbsps margarine
1/2 C. chopped onion
4 C. fresh broccoli florets, without the stems
6 large eggs
1 (8 oz.) pack cream of broccoli soup mix
1/3 C. cheddar cheese, shredded

1/3 C. parmesan cheese
1/2 C. whole milk
1 tsp white pepper
1 tsp salt

Directions

1. Set your oven to 350 degrees before doing anything else. Begin to stir fry your onions in margarine then combine in 1 tbsp of water and the broccoli. Fry everything for 7 mins with a low level of heat.

2. Get a bowl, combine: pepper, eggs, salt, soup mix, milk, and cheeses. Beat the mix until it is smooth then add in the broccoli mix and pour everything into a deep pie pan.

3. Cook the frittata in the oven for 22 mins then cut it into wedges once it has cooled. Enjoy.

The New Yorker
Frittata

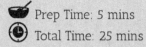 Prep Time: 5 mins

Total Time: 25 mins

Servings per Recipe: 4

Calories	304.2 kcal
Cholesterol	306.6mg
Sodium	619.5mg
Carbohydrates	17.0g
Protein	19.2g

Ingredients

4 slices turkey bacon, crumbled
1 1/2 C. potatoes, cubed
1 onion, chopped
6 eggs
1/2 C. water

1/2 tsp salt
1/4 tsp black pepper
2 C. frozen broccoli, thawed
3/4 C. cheddar cheese, shredded

Directions

1. Fry your bacon for 7 mins then combine in the onions and potatoes. Place a lid on the pan and let everything cook for 8 mins. Stir the mix at least twice as it cooks.
2. Now get a bowl and combine: 1/2 C. cheese, eggs, broccoli, 1/2 C. water, 1/4 tsp pepper, 1/2 tsp salt.
3. Whisk the mix until it is smooth then pour it into the pan. Place the lid back on the pan and cook everything with a medium level of heat for 9 mins.
4. Shut the heat and top the mix with the cheese and place the lid back on the pan.
5. Once the cheese has melted serve. Enjoy.

THE ATHENIAN
Frittata

🍳 Prep Time: 15 mins
🕐 Total Time: 1 hr 5 mins

Servings per Recipe: 8

Calories	411.0 kcal
Cholesterol	306.1mg
Sodium	553.2mg
Carbohydrates	28.5g
Protein	23.2g

Ingredients

5 potatoes, sliced
1/4 C. olive oil
1 C. onion, chopped
1/4 C. green pepper, chopped
3 garlic cloves, minced
4 C. frozen chopped broccoli
12 eggs, beaten
3/4 C. parmesan cheese, shredded

1/2 C. water
1 tsp dried basil leaves
1/2 tsp salt
1/2 tsp black pepper
1 1/2 C. Monterey jack cheese, shredded
(6 oz)

Directions

1. Set your oven to 350 degrees before doing anything else.
2. Stir fry your potatoes in oil for 12 mins then combine in the garlic, onion, and green pepper.
3. Stir the fry the mix until everything is soft then combine in the broccoli, place a lid on the pot, and let everything cook for 7 mins.
4. Layer your veggies into a casserole dish.
5. Get a bowl, combine: pepper, eggs, salt, parmesan, basil, and water. Whisk the mix until it is smooth then pour the eggs into the casserole dish evenly.
6. Top everything with the Monterey and cook the frittata in the oven for 27 mins. Enjoy.

Maggie's
Favorite Frittata

Prep Time: 30 mins
Total Time: 1 hr

Servings per Recipe: 6
Calories	304.4 kcal
Cholesterol	303.9mg
Sodium	423.8mg
Carbohydrates	3.3g
Protein	22.7g

Ingredients

1 C. broccoli floret
3/4 C. sliced fresh mushrooms
2 green onions, minced
1 tbsp butter
1 C. cooked turkey ham, cubed
8 eggs
1/4 C. water

1/4 C. Dijon mustard
1/2 tsp italian seasoning
1/4 tsp garlic salt
1 1/2 C. cheddar cheese, shredded (6 oz.)
1/2 C. tomatoes, chopped

Directions

1. Stir fry your onion, mushrooms, and broccoli until it is soft, in butter. Then remove everything from the pan. Get a bowl combine: garlic salt, eggs, Italian seasoning, water, and mustard.
2. Now set your oven to 375 degrees before doing anything else.
3. Stir the mix until it is smooth then add in the broccoli mix, tomatoes, and cheese.
4. Place everything into a casserole dish coated with nonstick spray and cook it all in the oven for 25 mins. Enjoy.

SOUP
of Broccoli, Potatoes, Onions, and Cheese

Prep Time: 15 mins
Total Time: 1 hr

Servings per Recipe: 6
Calories	183 kcal
Fat	8.1 g
Carbohydrates	21.7g
Protein	8.2 g
Cholesterol	14 mg
Sodium	297 mg

Ingredients

1 onion, diced
1 tbsp olive oil
2 heads broccoli, chopped
2 potatoes, peeled and cubed

4 C. chicken broth
4 oz. stilton cheese

Directions

1. Stir fry your onions in olive oil until see-through. Then add in your potatoes and broccoli and cook for 6 mins. Then add the broth and get the contents boiling. Once the broth is boiling set the heat to a lower level and let everything lightly boil for 23 mins with no cover.
2. Add the cheese after shutting the heat and let it melt. Use an immersion blender or regular food processor to blend the soup down to become smoother.
3. Then reheat it before serving.
4. Enjoy.

Broccoli Bake
Red Onions and Sage)

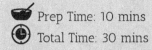 Prep Time: 10 mins
Total Time: 30 mins

Servings per Recipe: 4
Calories	97 kcal
Fat	7.1 g
Carbohydrates	7.3g
Protein	2.6 g
Cholesterol	0 mg
Sodium	546 mg

Ingredients

1 (12 oz.) bag broccoli florets
1/2 red onion, sliced
8 fresh sage leaves, torn
2 tbsps extra-virgin olive oil
1/2 tsp salt

1/2 tsp garlic salt
1/4 tsp ground black pepper

Directions

1. Cover a casserole dish or sheet for baking with foil and then set your oven to 400 degrees before doing anything else.
2. Layer your broccoli evenly throughout the dish and top with sage leaves and onions. Garnish all the veggies with olive oil and then black pepper, regular salt, and garlic salt.
3. Cook the veggies in the oven for 27 mins until slightly browned and crunchy.
4. Enjoy.

GARLIC
Broccoli and Cashews

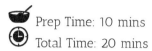
Servings per Recipe: 6

Calories	187 kcal
Fat	14.2 g
Carbohydrates	13.2g
Protein	5.1 g
Cholesterol	27 mg
Sodium	611 mg

Ingredients

1 1/2 lbs fresh broccoli, cut into bite size pieces
1/3 C. butter
1 tbsp brown sugar
3 tbsps soy sauce
2 tsps white vinegar

1/4 tsp ground black pepper
2 cloves garlic, minced
1/3 C. chopped salted cashews

Directions

1. Boil your broccoli in one inch of water for 8 mins. The remove all the liquid and place the broccoli on a plate.
2. Simultaneously as you are boiling the broccoli boil the following: garlic, butter, pepper, soy sauce, and vinegar. Once it is boiling shut the heat and add in the cashews.
3. Garnish your broccoli with the soy sauce mix and serve warm.
4. Enjoy.

Lemon
Broccoli Steamer

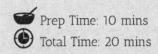 Prep Time: 10 mins

Total Time: 20 mins

Servings per Recipe: 4

Calories	120 kcal
Fat	9.1 g
Carbohydrates	8.8g
Protein	3.5 g
Cholesterol	23 mg
Sodium	100 mg

Ingredients

1 lb broccoli, separated into florets
2 tsps fresh lemon juice
2 tbsps water
3 tbsps butter
2 cloves garlic, minced

1 pinch salt
2 tsps lemon juice
1 tsp ground black pepper

Directions

1. Steam your broccoli for 16 mins in a frying pan with a lid on it in water with lemon juice (2 tsps).
2. Simultaneously stir fry your garlic with salt for 9 mins in butter.
3. Remove all the liquid from your broccoli and place it back in the pan, add the remaining lemon juice, and garlic mix. Garnish the florets with pepper.
4. Enjoy.

ARTISAN
Broccoli Soup II

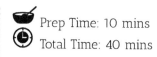 Prep Time: 10 mins
Total Time: 40 mins

Servings per Recipe: 12
Calories   265 kcal
Fat   18.2 g
Carbohydrates   15.1g
Protein   10 g
Cholesterol   56 mg
Sodium   1136 mg

Ingredients

1/2 C. butter
1 onion, chopped
1 (16 oz.) package frozen chopped
broccoli
4 (14.5 oz.) cans chicken broth
1 (1 lb) loaf processed cheese food,
cubed

2 C. milk
1 tbsp garlic powder
2/3 C. cornstarch
1 C. water

Directions

1. Get a bowl, mix until smooth: water and cornstarch.
2. Stir fry your onions in butter in a big pot and then add in your broccoli and broth. Let the broth and broccoli lightly boil for 16 mins. Then set the heat to low and pour in your cheese. Once the cheese has melted season everything with the garlic powder and pour in the milk.
3. Slowly stir and pour in your cornstarch mix. Let the soup cook for a bit more time (3 more mins).
4. Enjoy.

Enjoyable
Broccoli with Tomato Sauce

Prep Time: 5 mins
Total Time: 25 mins

Servings per Recipe: 2
Calories   291.4
Fat   4.7g
Cholesterol   0.0mg
Sodium   26.4mg
Carbohydrates   53.4g
Protein   9.9g

Ingredients

4 oz. pasta (Fusili works best!)
1/2 C. broccoli floret
2 - 2 1/2 C. water
FOR THE SAUCE
3 medium tomatoes, finely chopped
1/2 medium onion, finely chopped
1/2 tsp dried basil

1/2 tsp oregano
1/2 tsp dried parsley
1 1/2 tsp olive oil
salt
pepper
parmesan cheese, grated (optional)

Directions

1. In a large pan of lightly salted boiling water, cook the pasta for about 5-8 minutes.
2. Stir in the broccoli and cook for about 5-8 minutes.
3. Drain well, reserving about 1/2 C of the cooking liquid.
4. In a pan, heat the oil and sauté the onion till tender.
5. Stir in the tomatoes, reserved cooking liquid, salt and black pepper.
6. Simmer, covered for about 5 minutes.
7. Increase the heat to high and cook, uncovered for about 5 minutes.
8. Remove everything from the heat and immediately, stir in the pasta mixture and herbs.
9. Serve hot with a topping of Parmesan.

BROCCOLI
Sunflower Salad

Prep Time: 15 mins
Total Time: 4 hrs 30 mins

Servings per Recipe: 6
Calories	559 kcal
Fat	48.1 g
Carbohydrates	23.9g
Protein	12.9 g
Cholesterol	31 mg
Sodium	584 mg

Ingredients

10 slices bacon
1 head fresh broccoli, cut into bite size
pieces
1/4 C. red onion, diced
1/2 C. raisins
3 tbsps white wine vinegar
2 tbsps white sugar

1 C. mayonnaise
1 C. sunflower seeds

Directions

1. Stir fry your bacon until crispy then break it into pieces.
2. Get a bowl, combine: raisins, broccoli, and onions.
3. Get a 2nd bowl, combine: mayo, sugar, and vinegar.
4. Combine both bowls then place a covering of plastic around the bowl.
5. Put everything in the fridge for 4 hours.
6. Add in your bacon and stir the salad. Then add the sunflower seeds as a topping.
7. Enjoy.

Bacon
Broccoli Salad

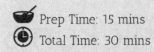 Prep Time: 15 mins

Total Time: 30 mins

Servings per Recipe: 12
Calories	273 kcal
Fat	24 g
Carbohydrates	7.3g
Protein	8.1 g
Cholesterol	35 mg
Sodium	543 mg

Ingredients

8 slices bacon
2 heads fresh broccoli, diced
1 1/2 C. sharp Cheddar cheese, shredded
1/2 large red onion, diced
1/4 C. red wine vinegar
1/8 C. white sugar
2 tsps ground black pepper

1 tsp salt
2/3 C. mayonnaise
1 tsp fresh lemon juice

Directions

1. Stir fry your bacon until it is fully done then break it into pieces.
2. Get a bowl, combine: onion, broccoli, bacon, and cheese.
3. Get a 2nd bowl, combine: lemon juice, red wine, mayo, sugar, salt, and pepper.
4. Combine both bowls then place a covering of plastic around the bowl and put everything in the fridge until it is chilled.
5. Enjoy.

GRILLED
Chicken Salad

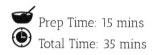

Prep Time: 15 mins
Total Time: 35 mins

Servings per Recipe: 6
Calories	239 kcal
Fat	11.1 g
Carbohydrates	17.5g
Protein	17.2 g
Cholesterol	43 mg
Sodium	69 mg

Ingredients

1/2 C. orange juice
1/2 C. white wine vinegar
1/4 C. olive oil
4 tbsps salt-free garlic and herb seasoning blend
1 1/2 tbsps white sugar
1 lb skinless, boneless chicken breast halves

1 head romaine lettuce- rinsed, dried and diced
1 (11 oz.) can mandarin oranges, drained
1 C. diced fresh broccoli
1 C. diced baby carrots

Directions

1. Get your grill hot and oil the grate.
2. Get a bowl, combine: sugar, orange juice, seasoning blend, olive oil, and vinegar.
3. Reserve half of a C. of this mix for later.
4. Cook your chicken for 7 mins, each side, on the grill, and coat the meat with the reserved mix often.
5. Get a 2nd bowl, combine: carrots, lettuce, broccoli, and oranges.
6. Julienne your chicken after it has been cooked then add it in with the orange mix and pour in the dressing. Enjoy.

Steamed
Broccoli Pesto

Prep Time: 15 mins
Total Time: 20 mins

Servings per Recipe: 8
Calories	112 kcal
Fat	10 g
Carbohydrates	3.3g
Protein	3.1 g
Cholesterol	2 mg
Sodium	54 mg

Ingredients

2 C. chopped broccoli florets
2 C. chopped fresh basil
1/4 C. extra-virgin olive oil
1/4 C. shaved Parmesan cheese
1/4 C. pine nuts
6 cloves garlic, peeled
2 tbsps vegetable broth, or more if needed

1 pinch cayenne pepper
salt and ground black pepper to taste

Directions

1. Arrange a steamer basket over a pan of water and bring to a boil on medium heat.
2. Place broccoli into a steamer basket and cook, covered for about 3-5 minutes or till tender.
3. Drain the broccoli well and transfer everything into a food processor with remaining ingredients and pulse till smooth.

CREAMY
Mushrooms with Shrimp Brown Rice

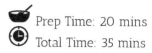 Prep Time: 20 mins
Total Time: 35 mins

Servings per Recipe: 6
Calories	317 kcal
Fat	6.3 g
Carbohydrates	43g
Protein	23.8 g
Cholesterol	173 mg
Sodium	1136 mg

Ingredients

2 C. instant brown rice
1 3/4 C. water
6 tbsps soy sauce
6 tbsps water
1/4 C. honey
2 tbsps cider vinegar
2 tbsps cornstarch
2 tbsps olive oil
2 cloves garlic, chopped

2 C. broccoli florets
1 C. baby carrots
1 small white onion, chopped
1/2 tsp black pepper
1 C. sliced fresh mushrooms
1 1/2 lbs uncooked medium shrimp, peeled and deveined

Directions

1. Get a bowl, mix: cornstarch, soy sauce, vinegar, honey, and water.
2. For 8 mins, in the microwave, cook your rice in 1 3/4 C. of water. Then stir it.
3. Stir fry your garlic in olive for 1 min then add in: black pepper, broccoli, onions, and carrots.
4. Continue frying for 7 more mins.
5. Then add the mushrooms and cook for 4 more mins.
6. Empty the pan.
7. Add in your cornstarch mix to the pan and cook it for 1.5 mins then add in your shrimp. Cook the shrimp for 4 mins before pouring in the veggies with the shrimp and reheating everything.
8. Serve the rice with the veggies and shrimp.
9. Enjoy.

Walnuts, Broccoli, and Cheddar Brown Rice

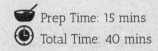 Prep Time: 15 mins

Total Time: 40 mins

Servings per Recipe: 4

Calories	368 kcal
Fat	22.9 g
Carbohydrates	30.4g
Protein	15.1 g
Cholesterol	37 mg
Sodium	643 mg

Ingredients

1/2 C. chopped walnuts
1 tbsp butter
1 onion, chopped
1/2 tsp minced garlic
1 C. uncooked instant brown rice
1 C. vegetable broth
1 lb fresh broccoli florets

1/2 tsp salt
1/8 tsp ground black pepper
1 C. shredded Cheddar cheese

Directions

1. Set your oven to 350 degrees before doing anything else.
2. Get a baking dish and toast your nuts in the oven for 9 mins.
3. Microwave the broccoli until soft, then add in some pepper and salt.
4. Now stir fry your garlic and onions in butter for 4 mins then add in the broth and rice. Get everything boiling, then place a lid on the pot, and let the contents, gently cook over a lower level of heat for 9 mins.
5. On each serving plate add a layer of rice, then some broccoli, then nuts, and finally some cheese.
6. Enjoy.

SPAGHETTI
Gazpacho

Prep Time: 15 mins
Total Time: 35 mins

Servings per Recipe: 6
Calories   155.8
Fat   2.1g
Cholesterol   4.4mg
Sodium   98.0mg
Carbohydrates   27.7g
Protein   7.0g

Ingredients

6 oz. spaghetti, uncooked
vegetable oil cooking spray
1 C. broccoli floret
1 C. carrot, thinly sliced
1 C. zucchini, sliced
1/4 C. onion, sliced
1 small yellow sweet pepper, julienned
1/2 C. cucumber, sliced

1/2 C. fresh mushrooms, sliced
1 small tomatoes, cut into 8 wedges
2 tbsps dry vermouth
6 tbsps grated parmesan cheese
1 tbsp fresh parsley, diced
1/4 tsp sweet red pepper flakes

Directions

1. Get your pasta boiling in water and salt for 9 mins then remove all the liquids.
2. Begin to stir fry your broccoli, carrots, zucchini, and onions, in a frying pan with nonstick spray for 6 mins then combine in the mushrooms, cucumbers, and yellow pepper.
3. Continue to stir fry everything for 6 more mins then combine in the vermouth, tomato, and pasta.
4. Stir the mix and cook everything for 3 dmins.
5. Top the pasta mix with the pepper flakes, cheese, and parsley.
6. Enjoy.

Orange
Chicken and Broccoli

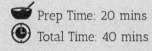 Prep Time: 20 mins
🕐 Total Time: 40 mins

Servings per Recipe: 4
Calories	380 kcal
Fat	14 g
Carbohydrates	33.1g
Protein	31.7 g
Cholesterol	68 mg
Sodium	938 mg

Ingredients

1/2 C. orange juice
3 tbsps soy sauce
3 cloves garlic, diced
1 tbsp grated orange zest
1 tsp ground ginger
1/2 tsp red pepper flakes (optional)
3 tbsps vegetable oil
4 skinless, boneless chicken breast halves, thinly sliced

1/2 C. chicken broth
2 tbsps cornstarch
1 (16 oz.) package frozen stir-fry vegetables
1 C. sugar snap peas
1 C. broccoli florets
1 C. sliced carrot

Directions

1. Get a bowl, combine: pepper flakes, orange juice, ginger, soy sauce, orange zest, and garlic.
2. Get your oil hot and then begin to stir fry your chicken and orange mix for 12 mins.
3. Get a 2nd bowl, combine: the cornstarch and broth.
4. Add this mix to the chicken, gradually, to make the sauce thicker.
5. Once the mix has reached a consistency that you prefer add: carrots, veggies, broccoli, and snap peas.
6. Continue frying and stirring the contents for 9 more mins.
7. Enjoy.

BEEF
and Broccoli

 Prep Time: 10 mins

Total Time: 1 hr 10 mins

Servings per Recipe: 4

Calories	665 kcal
Carbohydrates	104.6 g
Cholesterol	39 mg
Fat	13.8 g
Protein	30.5 g
Sodium	1594 mg

Ingredients

2 cups brown rice
4 cups water
2 tbsps cornstarch
2 tsps white sugar
6 tbsps soy sauce
1/4 cup white wine
1 tbsp minced fresh ginger
1 pound boneless beef round steak, cut into thin strips
1 tbsp vegetable oil
3 cups broccoli florets

2 carrots, thinly sliced
1 (6 ounce) package frozen pea pods, thawed
2 tbsps chopped onion
1 (8 ounce) can sliced water chestnuts, undrained
1 cup Chinese cabbage
2 large heads bok choy, chopped
1 tbsp vegetable oil

Directions

1. Get your rice boiling in water, set the heat to low, cover the pan, and let the rice cook for 40 mins until done.
2. Get a bowl, combine the following ingredients: soy sauce, cornstarch, wine, and sugar.
3. Mix everything evenly then add the ginger and beef to the marinade.
4. Get a wok and heat 1 tsp oil.
5. Begin to stir fry for 1 min: onions, broccoli, pea pods, and carrots.
6. Mix in: bok choy, Chinese cabbage, and the water chestnuts.
7. Place a lid on the pan and let everything fry for 4 mins.
8. Now remove everything from the pan and add in 1 tsp oil.
9. Begin to fry the beef for 4 mins. Then add the veggies back into the mix and continue frying everything for 3 more mins.
10. Enjoy with cooked brown rice.

Canadian
Asian Rice and Beef

Prep Time: 20 mins
Total Time: 1 hr 5 mins

Servings per Recipe: 6
Calories	507 kcal
Fat	18.7 g
Carbohydrates	59.2g
Protein	27.4 g
Cholesterol	61 mg
Sodium	649 mg

Ingredients

1 1/2 lbs beef top sirloin, thinly sliced
1/3 C. white sugar
1/3 C. rice wine vinegar
2 tbsps frozen orange juice concentrate
1 tsp salt
1 tbsp soy sauce
1 C. long grain rice
2 C. water

1/4 C. cornstarch
2 tsps orange zest
3 tbsps grated fresh ginger
1 1/2 tbsps minced garlic
8 broccoli florets, lightly steamed
2 C. oil for frying

Directions

1. Line a large baking sheet with paper towels.
2. Arrange the beef strips onto the prepared baking sheet in a single layer and refrigerate for about 30 minutes.
3. In a small bowl, mix together sugar, orange juice concentrate, vinegar, soy sauce and salt and keep aside.
4. In a pan, mix together water and rice and bring to a boil.
5. Reduce the heat to medium-low and simmer for about 20 minutes or till tender.
6. In a skillet, heat oil on medium-high heat.
7. Coat the beef with the cornstarch evenly and cook the beef in the skillet till golden brown and crispy and transfer onto a plate.
8. Discard the fat from the skillet, leaving 1 tbsp.
9. Add the garlic, ginger and orange zest and cook till fragrant.
10. Stir in the vinegar mixture and bring to a simmer and cook for about 5 minutes or till the sauce become thick. Stir in the beef and cook till heated completely.
11. Place the rice onto serving plates and top it with the beef mixture.
12. Serve with a garnishing of broccoli.

CHILLED
Creamy Broccoli Salad

Prep Time: 25 mins
Total Time: 2 hrs 50 mins

Servings per Recipe: 6
Calories	119 kcal
Fat	3.2 g
Carbohydrates	20.1g
Protein	4.6 g
Cholesterol	12 mg
Sodium	267 mg

Ingredients

3 C. broccoli florets
1/2 C. chopped red onion
1/4 C. sunflower seeds
1/2 C. chopped raisins
1/2 C. crumbled feta cheese
1/2 C. plain low-fat yogurt
1/4 C. light mayonnaise
2 tbsps white sugar

1 tbsp lemon juice
salt and pepper to taste

Directions

1. In a large bowl, mix together broccoli, onion, raisins, sunflower seeds and feta cheese.
2. In another bowl, add the remaining ingredients and beat till well combined.
3. Add the yogurt mixture into a salad bowl and toss to coat well.
4. Refrigerate, covered for at least 2 hours.

Cajun Mushrooms and Broccoli

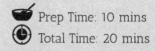 Prep Time: 10 mins

Total Time: 20 mins

Servings per Recipe: 6

Calories	90 kcal
Fat	6.3 g
Carbohydrates	7g
Protein	2.2 g
Cholesterol	10 mg
Sodium	302 mg

Ingredients

1 (10 oz.) package frozen chopped broccoli, thawed
1 C. fresh green beans, trimmed
2 tbsps butter
1 C. sliced fresh mushrooms

1 (15 oz.) can baby corn, drained
1 tbsp Cajun seasoning
1 tbsp olive oil

Directions

1. Get your green beans and broccoli boiling in water.
2. Let the veggies cook for 7 mins then remove all of the liquids.
3. Begin to stir fry your mushrooms in butter for 2 mins then combine in the corn and cook it for 2 more mins.
4. Add the beans and mushrooms then top everything with the olive oil and Cajun spice.
5. Enjoy.

BUFFALO
Soup II

Prep Time: 15 mins
Total Time: 40 mins

Servings per Recipe: 4
Calories   155 kcal
Fat   11.2 g
Carbohydrates   9.9g
Protein   5.4 g
Cholesterol   27 mg
Sodium   1058 mg

Ingredients

1 tsp unsalted butter
1/4 C. chopped celery
2 cloves garlic, chopped
1 tbsp all-purpose flour
3 1/2 C. chicken broth
1 1/2 C. chopped broccoli
1 1/2 C. cauliflower, chopped

2 tbsps peanut butter
1/4 tsp salt
1/4 tsp crushed red pepper flakes
2 green onions, chopped
1/4 C. heavy cream

Directions

1. Stir fry your garlic and celery in butter for 7 mins then add in the flour and stir everything again.
2. Let the mix fry for 60 secs then add in the pepper flakes, broth, salt, broccoli, peanut butter, and cauliflower.
3. Let the mix gently boil for 17 mins then add in the green onions and cream and stir everything again.
4. Enjoy.

New York Style
Pizza Bites

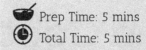 Prep Time: 5 mins

Total Time: 5 mins

Servings per Recipe: 8
Calories	306 kcal
Fat	19.5 g
Carbohydrates	22.7g
Protein	10.3 g
Cholesterol	30 mg
Sodium	439 mg

Ingredients

1 C. prepared spinach dip
1 (10 oz.) package prepared pizza crust
1 C. chopped broccoli
1 C. cooked and cubed chicken
1/3 C. chopped green onions

1 tomato, seeded and chopped

Directions

1. Coat your pizza crust with the spinach dip mix then layer your tomato, broccoli, green onions, and chicken over it.
2. Slice the pizza into slices then place them on a serving dish.
3. Enjoy.

CURRY
and Coconut Stir Fry

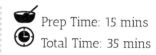

Prep Time: 15 mins
Total Time: 35 mins

Servings per Recipe: 4

Calories	372 kcal
Fat	24.2 g
Carbohydrates	16g
Protein	25.8 g
Cholesterol	59 mg
Sodium	387 mg

Ingredients

1 1/2 C. coconut milk
1 tbsp diced ginger
1 tbsp lime juice
1 tbsp fish sauce
1 tsp oyster sauce
2 tsps diced garlic
1/2 tsp chili-garlic sauce
2 tbsps white sugar

1 tbsp avocado oil
1 lb chicken breast, cut into bite-sized pieces
1/2 onion, sliced
1 1/2 tsps curry powder
2 C. broccoli florets

Directions

1. Get a bowl, combine: sugar, coconut milk, sriracha, lime juice, garlic, fish sauce, and oyster sauce.
2. Now begin to stir fry your chicken in hot avocado oil for 9 mins until it is fully done then place the chicken to the side.
3. Stir the onions and curry powder in the pan for 3 mins then add in the broccoli and cook the veggies for 4 mins before pouring in the coconut milk mix and getting everything boiling.
4. Once the mix is boiling set the heat to low and let the mix simmer for 4 mins.
5. Place the chicken back in the pan and place a lid on it. Let the mix cook for 5 mins.
6. Enjoy.

A Soup
from Vietnam

Prep Time: 15 mins
Total Time: 25 mins

Servings per Recipe: 4
Calories	159 kcal
Fat	2.3 g
Carbohydrates	29.2g
Protein	5.2 g
Cholesterol	5 mg
Sodium	991 mg

Ingredients

2 (14.5 oz.) cans chicken broth
2 star anise pods, or more to taste
3/4 tbsp ginger paste
1 tsp Sriracha
4 oz. tofu, cubed
1/2 C. broccoli florets

1/2 C. sliced mushrooms
1/4 C. chopped carrots
1/2 (8 oz.) package dried thin rice noodles
1 tbsp chopped green onion

Directions

1. Get the following boiling: sriracha, broth, ginger paste, and star anise.
2. Once the mix is boiling combine in: the carrots, tofu, mushrooms, and broccoli.
3. Let the mix cook for 9 mins.
4. Now begin get your noodles boiling in water.
5. Once the water is boiling shut the heat and place a lid on the pot.
6. Let the noodles sit for 6 mins then remove the liquids and run the noodles under some cool water.
7. Now take out the anise from the simmering mix.
8. Place your noodles in serving bowls and top them with the broth mix.
9. Place some green onions over everything.
10. Enjoy.

BROCCOLI
and Cheddar Quinoa

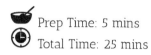 Prep Time: 5 mins

Total Time: 25 mins

Servings per Recipe: 4

Calories	299 kcal
Fat	12.3 g
Carbohydrates	32.9 g
Protein	14.8 g
Cholesterol	30 mg
Sodium	491 mg

Ingredients

2 C. chopped broccoli
1 3/4 C. vegetable broth
1 C. quinoa
1 C. shredded Cheddar cheese

salt and ground black pepper to taste

Directions

1. Boil, in a big pot: quinoa, broccoli, and broth.
2. Once boiling place a lid on the pot and lower the heat.
3. Let the quinoa gently boil for 17 mins. Then add your cheese.
4. Cook everything for 4 more mins until the cheese is melted and then add your preferred amount of pepper and salt.
5. Enjoy.

Broccoli
Casserole

🥣 Prep Time: 10 mins
🕐 Total Time: 50 mins

Servings per Recipe: 8
Calories   388.7
Cholesterol   46.8mg
Sodium   665.8mg
Carbohydrates   36.2g
Protein   10.9g

Ingredients

3 lbs fresh broccoli, chopped broccoli or 3 (10 oz.) packages frozen chopped broccoli
1/4 C. butter
1/4 C. flour
1 1/2 tbsps chicken stock powder
1/2 tsp salt
2 C. milk
6 tbsps butter
2/3 C. coarsely chopped walnuts or 2/3 C. slivered almonds

0.667 (8 oz.) packages herb seasoned stuffing mix
2/3 C. hot water

Directions

1. Set your oven to 400 degrees F before doing anything else and lightly coat a large casserole dish.
2. In a pan of salted boiling water, add the broccoli and cook till tender.
3. Drain well and chop roughly.
4. (If you are using frozen broccoli then prepare according to package's directions)
5. In a pan, whisk together 1/4 C. of butter, flour, stock powder and salt and then stir in the milk and cook till sauce becomes thick.
6. Meanwhile in a bowl add 1/3 C. of butter, seasoned stuffing packet and 2/3 C. of hot water and stir till butter melts completely and stir in the nuts.
7. Place the broccoli into the prepared casserole dish and place the sauce over the broccoli evenly.
8. Place the stuffing mixture on top evenly and gently, press down.
9. Cook everything in the oven for about 20-25 minutes.

VEGETABLE
Soup In Thailand

Prep Time: 15 mins
Total Time: 1 hr 30 mins

Servings per Recipe: 12
Calories	183 kcal
Carbohydrates	21.4 g
Cholesterol	< 1 mg
Fat	7.4 g
Protein	4.4 g
Sodium	749 mg

Ingredients

1 cup uncooked brown rice
2 cups water
3 tbsps olive oil
1 sweet onion, chopped
4 cloves garlic, minced
1/4 cup chopped fresh ginger root
1 cup chopped carrots
4 cups chopped broccoli
1 red bell pepper, diced
1 (14 ounce) can light coconut milk
6 cups vegetable broth
1 cup white wine
3 tbsps fish sauce
2 tbsps soy sauce
3 Thai chili peppers
2 tbsps chopped fresh lemon grass
1 tbsp Thai pepper garlic sauce
1 tsp saffron
3/4 cup plain yogurt
fresh cilantro, for garnish

Directions

1. Bring the mixture of rice and water to boil before turning the heat down to low and cooking for 45 minutes.
2. Cook ginger, carrots, garlic and onion in hot olive oil for about five minutes before you add broccoli, coconut milk, broth, wine, soy sauce, Thai chili peppers, red bell pepper, lemon grass, fish sauce, garlic sauce, and saffron into it and cook for another 25 minutes.
3. Now blend this soup in batches in a blender until you get the required smoothness.
4. Mix yoghurt and cooked rice very thoroughly with this soup.
5. Garnish with cilantro before you serve.

Sinigang Na Baka (Beef Based Veggie Soup)

🥣 Prep Time: 15 mins
🕐 Total Time: 1 hr

Servings per Recipe: 6
Calories	304 kcal
Carbohydrates	15 g
Cholesterol	51 mg
Fat	19.7 g
Protein	17.8 g
Sodium	1405 mg

Ingredients

2 tbsps canola oil
1 large onion, chopped
2 cloves garlic, chopped
1 pound beef stew meat, cut into 1 inch cubes
1 quart water
2 large tomatoes, diced
1/2 pound fresh green beans, rinsed and trimmed

1/2 medium head bok choy, cut into 1 1/2 inch strips
1 head fresh broccoli, cut into bite size pieces
1 (1.41 ounce) package tamarind soup base

Directions

1. Cook onion and garlic in hot oil and then add beef to get it brown.
2. Now add some water and bring it to a boil.
3. Turn the heat down to medium and cook for 30 minutes.
4. Cook for another 10 minutes after adding tomatoes and green beans.
5. Now add tamarind soup mix, bok choy and some broccoli into the mix and cook for 10 more minutes to get everything tender.

MIE GORENG
(Indonesian Fried Noodles)

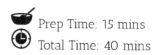

Prep Time: 15 mins
Total Time: 40 mins

Servings per Recipe: 6

Calories	356 kcal
Carbohydrates	34 g
Cholesterol	43 mg
Fat	14.3 g
Protein	22.7 g
Sodium	1824 mg

Ingredients

3 (3 ounce) packages ramen noodles (without flavor packets)
1 tbsp vegetable oil
1 pound skinless, boneless chicken breast halves, cut into strips
1 tsp olive oil
1 tsp garlic salt
1 pinch ground black pepper, or to taste
1 tbsp vegetable oil
1/2 cup chopped shallots
5 cloves garlic, chopped

1 cup shredded cabbage
1 cup shredded carrots
1 cup broccoli florets
1 cup sliced fresh mushrooms
1/4 cup soy sauce
1/4 cup sweet soy sauce (Indonesian kecap manis)
1/4 cup oyster sauce
salt and pepper to taste

Directions

1. Cook noodles in boiling water for about 3 minutes before running it through cold water to stop the process of cooking and draining all the water.
2. Coat chicken strips with olive oil, black pepper and garlic salt before cooking it in hot oil for about 5 minutes or until you see that the chicken is no longer pink.
3. Now add garlic and shallots, and cook them until you see that they are turning brown.
4. Now add all the vegetables into the pan and cook it for another five minutes or until you see that the vegetables are tender.
5. Add the mixture of noodles, soy sauce, oyster sauce and sweet soy sauce into the pan containing chicken and vegetables.
6. Sprinkle some salt and pepper before serving.
7. Enjoy.

Chicken
& Broccoli

Prep Time: 10 mins
Total Time: 35 mins

Servings per Recipe: 6
Calories	170 kcal
Carbohydrates	9.8 g
Cholesterol	33 mg
Fat	7.9 g
Protein	16.2 g
Sodium	418 mg

Ingredients

12 ounces boneless, skinless chicken breast halves, cut into bite-sized pieces
1 tbsp oyster sauce
2 tbsps dark soy sauce
3 tbsps vegetable oil
2 cloves garlic, chopped
1 large onion, cut into rings
1/2 cup water
1 tsp ground black pepper
1 tsp white sugar
1/2 medium head bok choy, chopped
1 small head broccoli, chopped
1 tbsp cornstarch, mixed with equal parts water

Directions

1. Mix chicken, soy sauce and oyster sauce in large bowl and set it aside for later use.
2. Cook garlic and onion in hot oil for about three minutes before adding chicken mixture and cooking it for another ten minutes.
3. Now add water, sugar, broccoli, pepper and bok choy, and cook it for another ten minutes.
4. In the end, add cornstarch mixture and cook it for another 5 minutes to get the sauce thick.
5. Enjoy.

CAP CAI
(Indo-Chinese Shrimp Veggie Salad)

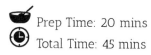 Prep Time: 20 mins

Total Time: 45 mins

Servings per Recipe: 4

Calories	250 kcal
Carbohydrates	18.7 g
Cholesterol	106 mg
Fat	11.9 g
Protein	18.9 g
Sodium	819 mg

Ingredients

3 tbsps vegetable oil
4 cloves garlic, minced
1 onion, thinly sliced
10 ounces peeled and deveined medium shrimp (30 - 40 per pound)
1 head bok choy, chopped
1 1/2 cups chopped broccoli
1 1/2 cups chopped cauliflower
1 large carrot, thinly sliced at an angle
3 green onions, chopped
2/3 cup water

2 tbsps cornstarch
2 tbsps fish sauce
2 tbsps oyster sauce
1 tsp white sugar
1/2 tsp ground black pepper
salt to taste

Directions

1. Cook onion and garlic in hot oil for about five minutes before adding shrimp, broccoli, cauliflower, bok choy, carrot, water and green onion, and cook this for about 15 minutes or until you see that all the vegetables are tender.

2. Add a mixture of fish sauce and cornstarch, to the cap cai and also some oyster sauce, pepper and sugar.

3. Mix it thoroughly and add some salt according to your taste before serving.

Pho Soup

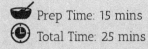 Prep Time: 15 mins

Total Time: 25 mins

Servings per Recipe: 6

Calories	159 kcal
Carbohydrates	29.2 g
Cholesterol	5 mg
Fat	2.3 g
Protein	5.2 g
Sodium	991 mg

Ingredients

2 (14.5 ounce) cans chicken broth
2 star anise pods, or more to taste
3/4 tbsp ginger paste
1 tsp sriracha hot sauce, or more to taste
4 ounces tofu, cubed
1/2 cup broccoli florets

1/2 cup sliced mushrooms
1/4 cup chopped carrots
1/2 (8 ounce) package dried thin rice noodles
1 tbsp chopped green onion

Directions

1. Bring the mixture of chicken broth, ginger paste, star anise and sriracha hot sauce to boil before adding carrots, tofu, mushrooms and broccoli, and cooking it for seven minutes or until you see that the vegetables are tender.

2. Put noodles in hot water for about four minutes and drain.

3. After removing star anise from the broth mixture, add this mixture on top of noodles in serving bowls.

4. Serve.

CHICKEN
Ramen Stir-Fry

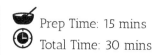 Prep Time: 15 mins
Total Time: 30 mins

Servings per Recipe: 2
Calories	438 kcal
Carbohydrates	47.6 g
Cholesterol	65 mg
Fat	14.1 g
Protein	31.9 g
Sodium	1118 mg

Ingredients

1 1/2 cups hot water
1 (3 ounce) package Oriental-flavor ramen noodle soup mix
2 tsps vegetable oil, divided
8 ounces skinless, boneless chicken breast halves, cut into 2-inch strips
2 cups broccoli florets
1 cup sliced onion wedges
2 cloves garlic, minced
1 cup fresh bean sprouts
1/2 cup water

1/2 cup sliced water chestnuts
1 tsp soy sauce
1 tsp oyster sauce
1/4 tsp chili-garlic sauce (such as Sriracha®), or to taste
1 roma tomato, cut into wedges

Directions

1. Cook ramen noodles in boiling water for about 2 minutes and drain it with the help of colander.

2. Now cook chicken in hot oil for about 5 minutes and set it aside in a bowl.

3. In the same skillet; Cook broccoli, garlic and onion for about three minutes before adding noodles, water, oyster sauce, chili garlic sauce, water chestnuts, bean sprouts, soy sauce and seasoning from the ramen noodle package.

4. Cook all this for about 5 minutes before adding tomato wedges and cooking it for three more minutes.

Nutty
Ramen Salad

Prep Time: 20 mins
Total Time: 35 mins

Servings per Recipe: 12
Calories	395 kcal
Carbohydrates	28.9 g
Cholesterol	23 mg
Fat	28.8 g
Protein	8 g
Sodium	252 mg

Ingredients

1 (16 ounce) package coleslaw mix
8 green onions, chopped
1/2 cup butter or margarine
1 head fresh broccoli, cut into florets
2 (3 ounce) packages chicken flavored
ramen noodles
1 cup slivered almonds

1 cup unsalted sunflower seeds
1/2 cup white sugar
1/4 cup apple cider vinegar
1/2 cup vegetable oil
1 tsp soy sauce

Directions

1. Mix broccoli, coleslaw mix and green onion in a bowl and set it aside.
2. Cook the mixture of ramen noodles, sunflower seeds, seasoning packets and almonds in hot butter for about eight minutes or until the nuts are toasted.
3. Pour the mixture of sugar, soy sauce and oil over the mixture of noodles mixture and slaw mixture.
4. Mix it very thoroughly before serving.

ASIAN STYLE
Broccoli and Chicken

Prep Time: 10 mins
Total Time: 30 mins

Servings per Recipe: 4
Calories   156 kcal
Fat   6.2 g
Carbohydrates   10.9g
Protein   15.9 g
Cholesterol   36 mg
Sodium   606 mg

Ingredients

3 C. broccoli florets
1 tbsp olive oil
2 skinless, boneless chicken breast
halves - cut into 1 inch strips
1/4 C. sliced green onions
4 cloves garlic, thinly sliced
1 tbsp hoisin sauce
1 tbsp chili paste
1 tbsp low sodium soy sauce

1/2 tsp ground ginger
1/4 tsp crushed red pepper
1/2 tsp salt
1/2 tsp black pepper
1/8 C. chicken stock

Directions

1. With a steamer insert and 2 inches of water steam your broccoli for 6 mins.
2. Now stir fry: garlic, chicken, and green onions until the chicken is fully done.
3. Add in with the chicken the following: chicken stock, soy sauce, black pepper, ginger, salt, red pepper, chili paste, and hoisin.
4. Get the broth boiling and let it continue boiling for 4 mins. Now add in your broccoli and let it cook until the sauce thickens for about 1 more min.
5. Enjoy with jasmine rice.

Peanuts and Ramen Broccoli Salad

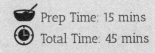 Prep Time: 15 mins

Total Time: 45 mins

Servings per Recipe: 6

Calories	562 kcal
Fat	34.4 g
Carbohydrates	52.3g
Protein	16.5 g
Cholesterol	0 mg
Sodium	356 mg

Ingredients

1 (16 oz.) package broccoli coleslaw mix
2 (3 oz.) packages chicken flavored ramen noodles
1 bunch green onions, chopped
1 C. unsalted peanuts
1 C. sunflower seeds
1/2 C. white sugar

1/4 C. vegetable oil
1/3 C. cider vinegar

Directions

1. Get a bowl, mix: green onions, vinegar, sugar, crushed ramen and its seasoning, oil, and slaw.
2. Toss the slaw mix and then add seeds and peanuts.
3. Enjoy chilled after 20 mins in the fridge.

HONEY
Mustard Chicken and Broccoli

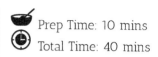

Prep Time: 10 mins
Total Time: 40 mins

Servings per Recipe: 16
Calories	183 kcal
Fat	12.7 g
Carbohydrates	7.8g
Protein	8.9 g
Cholesterol	27 mg
Sodium	275 mg

Ingredients

2 C. chopped, cooked chicken meat
2 C. fresh chopped broccoli
1/2 C. chopped onion
2 tbsps honey
1/2 C. chopped green bell pepper
1 1/2 C. shredded Cheddar cheese
1/2 C. mayonnaise
2 tbsps Dijon-style prepared mustard
salt and pepper to taste

1 tbsp minced garlic
1 (8 oz.) package refrigerated crescent rolls

Directions

1. Set your oven to 400 degrees before doing anything else.
2. Get a bowl, mix: garlic, chicken, pepper, broccoli, salt, honey, onions, mustard, bell peppers, mayo, and cheese.
3. Line a baking dish or casserole dish with foil.
4. Get a 2nd bowl and place it upside down on the dish and roll out your dough around the top of the bowl.
5. Add some chicken to the rolled out dough and fold to form a roll around the mix.
6. Repeat for any remaining dough or mixture.
7. Place the roll on the sheet and cook in the oven for 27 mins.
8. Enjoy.

Bacon, Tomatoes, and Tortellini Broccoli Salad

Prep Time: 15 mins
Total Time: 1 hr 30 mins

Servings per Recipe: 10
Calories   349 kcal
Fat   18.2 g
Carbohydrates   33.6g
Protein   13.9 g
Cholesterol   47 mg
Sodium   736 mg

Ingredients

2 (9 oz.) packages refrigerated three-cheese tortellini
1 lb bacon
4 C. chopped broccoli
1 pint grape tomatoes, halved

2 green onions, finely chopped
1 C. bottled coleslaw dressing

Directions

1. Boil your pasta in water and salt for about 8 mins then remove all the liquid and place the pasta in the fridge and in a bowl for 35 mins.
2. Fry your bacon for 9 to 12 mins, remove excess oils and then place the bacon on paper towels. Now break it into pieces after a good amount of grease has been absorbed by the towels.
3. Get a big bowl, toss: green onions, pasta, tomatoes, dressing, broccoli, and bacon.
4. Place the mix in the fridge for 10 to 20 min until fully chilled then serve.
5. Enjoy.

ARTISAN
Broccoli Soup

Prep Time: 15 mins
Total Time: 30 mins

Servings per Recipe: 4
Calories	449 kcal
Fat	33 g
Carbohydrates	18.9 g
Protein	20.6 g
Cholesterol	100 mg
Sodium	523 mg

Ingredients

1 C. sliced carrots
2 C. chopped broccoli
1 C. water
1 tsp chicken bouillon granules
1/4 C. chopped onion
1/4 C. butter
1/4 C. all-purpose flour

1/4 tsp ground black pepper
2 C. milk
2 C. shredded sharp Cheddar cheese

Directions

1. Get the following boiling in a large pot: bouillon, carrots, water, and broccoli.
2. Once the contents are boiling place a lid on the pan and let the contents simmer over a low heat for 7 mins. Place everything to the side.
3. In another big pot fry your onions in butter until see-through and add in pepper and flour. Let this cook for 1 min while stirring. Then add in your milk. Get everything boiling and then add in your cheese once the cheese has fully melted, pour in your vegetables and liquid.
4. Get the mix hot and then serve in bowls.
5. Enjoy.

Brown Rice,
Walnuts, and Cheddar Broccoli Bake

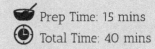 Prep Time: 15 mins

Total Time: 40 mins

Servings per Recipe: 4

Calories	368 kcal
Fat	22.9 g
Carbohydrates	30.4g
Protein	15.1 g
Cholesterol	37 mg
Sodium	643 mg

Ingredients

1/2 C. chopped walnuts
1 tbsp butter
1 onion, chopped
1/2 tsp minced garlic
1 C. uncooked instant brown rice
1 C. vegetable broth
1 lb fresh broccoli florets

1/2 tsp salt
1/8 tsp ground black pepper
1 C. shredded Cheddar cheese

Directions

1. Set your oven to 350 degrees before doing anything else. Once heated, toast your walnuts in a casserole dish for 7 mins.
2. Stir fry your garlic and onions in butter for 5 mins and then add the broth and rice.
3. Once the contents are boiling, lower the heat and place a lid on the pan.
4. Let the contents cook for 10 mins with a light simmer.
5. Simultaneously microwave your broccoli after topping it with pepper and salt until soft.
6. Create your individual serving plates by adding some rice and then some broccoli and walnuts with a final layer of cheese.
7. Enjoy hot.

BROCCOLI
Tots

Prep Time: 10 mins
Total Time: 20 mins

Servings per Recipe: 12
Calories	113 kcal
Fat	5.1 g
Carbohydrates	12.6 g
Protein	4.5 g
Cholesterol	27 mg
Sodium	284 mg

Ingredients

3 tbsps prepared Dijon-style mustard
4 tbsps honey
2 C. broccoli florets
1 C. shredded Cheddar cheese
1 egg
1 C. milk
1/2 C. sifted all-purpose flour

1/2 tsp baking powder
1/2 tsp salt
1/2 tsp vegetable oil
1/2 C. vegetable oil for frying

Directions

1. Get a bowl, mix: honey and mustard.
2. Get a deep fryer or large skillet and heat your oil to 375 degrees for frying later.
3. Dice your broccoli and then blend them in a blender and place everything in a 2nd bowl with cheese.
4. Get a 3rd bowl, beat with .5 tsp of oil: milk, salt, whisked eggs, baking powder, and flour.
5. Combine the broccoli with the milk and flour mix and stir to form a thick batter.
6. Fry dollops of the broccoli mix until golden.
7. Once all the bite sized broccoli pieces have been fried, garnish them with the honey sauce.
8. Enjoy as a unique appetizer.

Easy
Broccoli and Quinoa

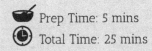 Prep Time: 5 mins
 Total Time: 25 mins

Servings per Recipe: 4
Calories   299 kcal
Fat   12.3 g
Carbohydrates   32.9g
Protein   14.8 g
Cholesterol   30 mg
Sodium   491 mg

Ingredients

2 C. chopped broccoli
1 3/4 C. vegetable broth
1 C. quinoa
1 C. shredded Cheddar cheese

salt and ground black pepper to taste

Directions

1. Boil the following in a large pot: quinoa, veggie broth, and broccoli.
2. Once the broth is boiling set the heat to low and place a lid on the pot.
3. Let the contents cook for 17 mins.
4. Add in your cheese and put the lid back on.
5. Let everything cook for 4 more mins then add pepper and salt.
6. Enjoy.

BROCCOLI
and Cheddar Quiche

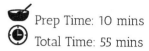

Prep Time: 10 mins
Total Time: 55 mins

Servings per Recipe: 8
Calories	401 kcal
Carbohydrates	10.6 g
Cholesterol	202 mg
Fat	32.4 g
Protein	19.3 g
Sodium	796 mg

Ingredients

1 cup sliced fresh mushrooms
1 cup chopped onions
1 cup chopped broccoli
5 eggs
1/3 cup MIRACLE WHIP Calorie-Wise Dressing
1/3 cup milk

1 cup KRAFT Double Cheddar Shredded Cheese Light
1 frozen deep-dish pie crust (9 inch pie)

Directions

1. Preheat your oven to 400 degrees F and put some oil over the quiche dish.
2. Cook all the vegetables in hot oil over medium heat for about 5 minutes.
3. Now add this mixture of vegetables and cheese into the mixture of eggs, milk and dressing.
4. Put this into the baking dish
5. Bake in the preheated oven for about 45 minutes or until the top of the quiche is golden brown in color.

Asian Style
Broccoli with Beef

Prep Time: 15 mins
Total Time: 30 mins

Servings per Recipe: 4
Calories	178 kcal
Fat	3.2 g
Carbohydrates	19 g
Protein	19.2 g
Cholesterol	39 mg
Sodium	755 mg

Ingredients

1/4 C. all-purpose flour
1 (10.5 oz.) can beef broth
2 tbsps white sugar
2 tbsps soy sauce
1 lb boneless round steak, cut into bite size pieces

1/4 tsp chopped fresh ginger root
1 clove garlic, minced
4 C. chopped fresh broccoli

Directions

1. Get a bowl, combine until smooth: soy sauce, flour, sugar, and broth.
2. Now stir fry your beef for 5 mins and add the soy sauce mix, broccoli, garlic, and ginger. Get the contents simmering with a high heat and then lower it.
3. Let the soy sauce mix get thick while lightly boiling for about 7 to 12 mins.
4. Enjoy with jasmine rice.

ASIAN STYLE
Broccoli and Beef

 Prep Time: 15 mins
Total Time: 1 hr

Servings per Recipe: 4
Calories	303 kcal
Fat	7.1 g
Carbohydrates	35.1g
Protein	26.4 g
Cholesterol	46 mg
Sodium	1533 mg

Ingredients

2 tbsps low-sodium soy sauce
2 tbsps fat-free Italian dressing
1 tsp cornstarch
1 tbsp minced garlic
1 tsp ground ginger
3/4 lb round steak, cut into strips
6 C. water

5 cubes beef bouillon
4 oz. linguine pasta, uncooked
1/2 C. fat free beef broth
1 C. fresh mushrooms, sliced
1/2 C. sliced green onion
1 lb broccoli, separated into florets

Directions

1. Get a bowl, combine: ginger, soy sauce, garlic, steak, cornstarch, and dressing.
2. Cover the bowl with plastic wrap and place it in the fridge for 20 mins.
3. Simultaneously while the steak is soaking boil your pasta in water and bouillon for 9 mins. The remove the excess liquid.
4. Stir fry your beef for 3 mins until browned and cooked through and add in the broth, onions, and mushrooms. Get the broth boiling and then place a lid on the pan and let the contents lightly boil for 7 mins.
5. Take off the lid and input your broccoli and stir the mix until you find that the broccoli is a bit soft and bright in colour.
6. Finally combine the beef and sauce with the pasta and stir to evenly coat.
7. Enjoy.

The Best
Chicken Stir-Fry I Know

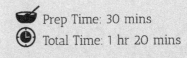

Prep Time: 30 mins
Total Time: 1 hr 20 mins

Servings per Recipe: 6	
Calories	700 kcal
Carbohydrates	76.7 g
Cholesterol	161 mg
Fat	12.1 g
Protein	67.7 g
Sodium	1790 mg

Ingredients

2 cups white rice
4 cups water
2/3 cup soy sauce
1/4 cup brown sugar
1 tbsp cornstarch
1 tbsp minced fresh ginger
1 tbsp minced garlic
1/4 tsp red pepper flakes
3 skinless, boneless chicken breast halves, thinly sliced

1 tbsp sesame oil
1 green bell pepper, cut into matchsticks
1 (8 ounce) can sliced water chestnuts, drained
1 head broccoli, broken into florets
1 cup sliced carrots
1 onion, cut into large chunks
1 tbsp sesame oil

Directions

1. Get a saucepan. Add rice and water. Get water boiling with high heat. Once boiling lower heat to low. Cover and let rice cook for 25 to 30 mins.
2. Get a small bowl and mix the following ingredients: corn starch, soy sauce, and brown sugar.
3. Combine with the corn starch: red pepper, ginger, and garlic.
4. This is your marinade. Cover chicken with it for 30 mins.
5. Get a wok heat 1 tbsp of sesame oil hot with high heat.
6. Fry the following ingredients for 6 mins: onion, bell pepper, carrots, water chestnuts, and broccoli. Place aside.
7. Add 1 tbsp of sesame oil to your frying pan and get it hot.
8. Grab your chicken and separate the meat and marinade.
9. Fry the chicken for 3 mins on each side until almost cooked but not 100% done.
10. Add veggies to the chicken and stir fry everything for 10 mins.
11. Enjoy.

BEEF
Stir-Fry I

Prep Time: 10 mins
Total Time: 1 hr 10 mins

Servings per Recipe: 4
Calories	665 kcal
Carbohydrates	104.6 g
Cholesterol	39 mg
Fat	13.8 g
Protein	30.5 g
Sodium	1594 mg

Ingredients

2 cups brown rice
4 cups water
2 tbsps cornstarch
2 tsps white sugar
6 tbsps soy sauce
1/4 cup white wine
1 tbsp minced fresh ginger
1 pound boneless beef round steak, cut into thin strips
1 tbsp vegetable oil
3 cups broccoli florets

2 carrots, thinly sliced
1 (6 ounce) package frozen pea pods, thawed
2 tbsps chopped onion
1 (8 ounce) can sliced water chestnuts, undrained
1 cup Chinese cabbage
2 large heads bok choy, chopped
1 tbsp vegetable oil

Directions

1. Get a large pan. Add water, heat until boiling. Add rice. Lower heat to low. Cover the pan. Let the rice cook for 40 mins until done.
2. Get a bowl combine the following ingredients: soy sauce, cornstarch, wine, and sugar. Mix evenly then add ginger. Add beef to this marinade.
3. Get wok. Heat 1 tsp oil for frying. Stir fry for 1 min: onions, broccoli, pea pods, and carrots.
4. Mix in: bok choy, Chinese cabbage, and water chestnuts. Place a lid on the pan and let fry for 4 mins.
5. Remove everything from pan.
6. Add 1 tsp oil to pan and fry beef for 4 mins. Add veggies back and fry for 3 mins.
7. Enjoy with rice.

Sesame Veggie Stir-Fry

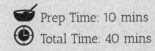
Prep Time: 10 mins
Total Time: 40 mins

Servings per Recipe: 4
Calories	191 kcal
Carbohydrates	16.9 g
Cholesterol	0 mg
Fat	11.4 g
Protein	7 g
Sodium	1258 mg

Ingredients

1 pound broccoli
1/4 pound fresh snow peas, strings removed
1 red onion, sliced
3 tbsps sesame oil
1 red bell pepper, cut into 1/4-inch strips
2 tsps minced garlic
1/4 cup Kikkoman Less Sodium Soy Sauce
1/2 tbsp sesame seeds

Directions

1. Cut your broccoli so that its stem is only 1 inch in length.
2. Any stem that is left should be diced for faster cooking.
3. Get a pot and boil some water in it. Once boiling add broccoli and snow peas let them boil for about 1 min.
4. Rinse them under cool water to stop cooking process plate them for later.
5. Get a frying pan and heat sesame oil.
6. Stir fry the following for 1 min: snow peas, broccoli, red bell pepper, red onion, and some garlic.
7. Now combine with the veggies your soy sauce and stir fry for about 2 mins.
8. Finally add some sesame seeds and let everything cool before serving.
9. Enjoy.

INDIAN
Stir-Fry

 Prep Time: 15 mins
Total Time: 30 mins

Servings per Recipe: 1
Calories	262 kcal
Carbohydrates	13.2 g
Cholesterol	148 mg
Fat	15.2 g
Protein	21 g
Sodium	193 mg

Ingredients

1 tbsp vegetable oil, or to taste
1/4 onion, chopped
1 clove garlic, minced
1 tsp curry powder, or to taste
1/4 tsp ground cumin
salt and ground black pepper to taste
1 cup chopped asparagus

1/2 cup broccoli florets
2 tbsps water
3 1/2 ounces uncooked medium shrimp, peeled and deveined

Directions

1. Get a frying and pan and with a medium level of heat get your oil hot.
2. Stir fry your onions and garlic for 7 mins.
3. Combine the following seasonings with onions: pepper, salt, cumin, and curry powder.
4. Then mix into the onions your broccoli and asparagus.
5. Cover the veggies with some water and cook until everything is soft for about 4 mins.
6. Finally add shrimp to the veggies and stir fry until the shrimp are pink
7. Enjoy.

Ragin'
Cajun Stir-Fry

Prep Time: 15 mins
Total Time: 45 mins

Servings per Recipe: 6

Calories	584 kcal
Carbohydrates	95 g
Cholesterol	40 mg
Fat	15.5 g
Protein	17.9 g
Sodium	769 mg

Ingredients

4 cups water
1/4 tsp salt
2 tbsps butter
3 dried red chilies, broken into several pieces
2 cups uncooked white rice
1 tbsp sesame oil
2 garlic cloves, minced
2 tbsps soy sauce, divided
1 skinless, boneless chicken breast half, diced

1 tsp dried basil
1 tsp ground white pepper
1/2 tsp dry ground mustard
1 pinch ground turmeric
1 tbsp butter
1 1/2 cups broccoli florets
1 cup diced green bell pepper
1 cup diced red bell pepper
1/2 cup diced onion
1 tsp lemon juice

Directions

1. Get a pot and with a high level of heat mix the following: red chili peppers, 2 tbsps of butter, water, and salt. Let everything begin to simmer before continuing.
2. Once boiling add rice and bring the heat down to a low level let the rice cook down until soft for about 20 mins, stirring sometimes.
3. Get a frying pan heat sesame oil. Stir fry with some garlic until aromatic in the oil and pour in half of your soy sauce after 1 min.
4. Stir fry the chicken in the soy sauce and garlic with the following ingredients for 8 mins: turmeric, basil, dry mustard, and white pepper.
5. Add the other half of the soy sauce.
6. Stir fry 1 tablespoon of butter with onion, green pepper, and broccoli in another frying pan for 10 mins until everything is soft.
7. Add some lemon juice to these veggies.
8. Finally mix the veggies with the chicken before letting everything cool down. Enjoy.

MAGGIE'S
Favorite Shrimp Stir-Fry

Prep Time: 30 mins
Total Time: 45 mins

Servings per Recipe: 4
Calories	337 kcal
Carbohydrates	39 g
Cholesterol	166 mg
Fat	9.7 g
Protein	24.3 g
Sodium	756 mg

Ingredients

1/2 cup water
2 tbsps ketchup
2 tbsps soy sauce
2 1/2 tsps cornstarch
1 tsp honey
1 tsp Asian (toasted) sesame oil
1/4 tsp red pepper flakes
3/4 pound cooked shrimp
2 tbsps vegetable oil
2 cloves garlic, crushed

1 thin slice fresh ginger root
1 small head broccoli, broken into florets
1 red bell pepper, sliced
1 small onion, halved and sliced
1 small yellow squash, sliced
1 small zucchini, sliced
4 mushrooms, quartered
2 cups hot cooked rice

Directions

1. Get a bowl and combine the following: red pepper flakes, water, and sesame oil, ketchup, honey, cornstarch and soy sauce.
2. Add shrimp. Evenly coat.
3. Get wok and heat veggie oil.
4. Stir fry ginger and garlic for 1 min.
5. Remove the garlic and ginger from the oil and throw it away.
6. Stir fry the following in the seasoned oil for 5 mins: red bell peppers, mushrooms, broccoli, zucchini, onion, and yellow squash.
7. Combine shrimp, veggies, and all liquid. Stir fry over high heat for 5 mins.
8. Serve with rice.
9. Enjoy.

Chicken
and Spaghetti Stir Fry

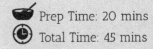 Prep Time: 20 mins
Total Time: 45 mins

Servings per Recipe: 4
Calories	403 kcal
Fat	8.7 g
Carbohydrates	57g
Protein	24.7 g
Cholesterol	34 mg
Sodium	566 mg

Ingredients

8 oz. spaghetti
2 cloves crushed garlic
2 tbsps olive oil
1 onion, sliced into thin rings
2 skinless, boneless chicken breast halves
- cut into bite-size pieces
2 C. broccoli florets

2 C. cauliflower florets
2 C. julienned carrots
salt to taste
ground black pepper to taste
2 tbsps soy sauce

Directions

1. Boil your pasta in water and salt for 9 mins then remove all the liquids.
2. At the same time, as the pasta cooks, begin to stir fry your garlic for 2 mins in oil.
3. Then add the onions and continue cooking the onions until they are tender.
4. Now add the chicken and fry the contents until the chicken is fully done.
5. Once the chicken is done add: the carrots, cauliflower, and broccoli.
6. Let everything cook for 7 mins then top the mix with pepper, salt, and soy sauce.
7. Combine the veggies with the pasta and serve.
8. Enjoy.

VEGGIE
Cheese Bites

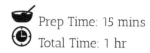

Prep Time: 15 mins
Total Time: 1 hr

Servings per Recipe: 6

Calories	530 kcal
Carbohydrates	23.8 g
Cholesterol	196 mg
Fat	36.5 g
Protein	28.2 g
Sodium	1068 mg

Ingredients

1/4 cup butter
2 (10 ounce) packages frozen broccoli florets, thawed and drained
1 pound shredded sharp Cheddar cheese
1 cup milk
1 cup all-purpose flour

3 eggs
1 tsp baking powder
1 tsp salt
ground black pepper to taste

Directions

1. Preheat your oven at 350 degrees F and put some oil over the quiche dish.
2. Combine broccoli, milk, flour, eggs, baking powder, salt, Cheddar cheese and black pepper in medium sized bowl.
3. Pour this mixture in the quiche dish over melted butter.
4. Bake in the preheated oven for about 45 minutes or until the top of the quiche is golden brown in color.
5. Serve.

Broccoli, Lentils, and Tomato Quiche

Prep Time: 15 mins
Total Time: 1 hr 30 mins

Servings per Recipe: 8
Calories	165 kcal
Fat	9.1 g
Carbohydrates	12.4g
Protein	9.7 g
Cholesterol	103 mg
Sodium	392 mg

Ingredients

1 C. diced onion
2 tbsps olive oil
1/2 C. dried lentils
2 C. water
2 C. broccoli florets
1 C. diced fresh tomatoes

4 eggs, beaten
1 C. milk
1 tsp salt
ground black pepper to taste
2 tsps Italian seasoning
1/2 C. shredded Cheddar cheese (optional)

Directions

1. Set your oven to 375 degrees before doing anything else.
2. Coat your pie crust with olive oil and then layer the onions in it.
3. Cook the crust in the oven for 17 mins.
4. Get your water and lentils boiling.
5. Let the lentils cook for 22 mins. Then remove any excess liquids.
6. Layer the broccoli on over the lentils and place the lid on the pot and cook the mix for 7 mins.
7. Enter the tomatoes, broccoli, and lentils into the pie crust and stir the mix.
8. Add the cheese as well and stir again.
9. Get a bowl, combine: Italian seasoning, eggs, pepper, milk, and salt.
10. Enter this mix into your pie crust as well.
11. Cook everything in the oven for 50 mins then let the quiche cool for 10 mins.
12. Enjoy.

MAGGIE'S
Easy Cauliflower Soup

Prep Time: 15 mins
Total Time: 50 mins

Servings per Recipe: 12
Calories   74 kcal
Fat   0.7 g
Carbohydrates   13.5g
Protein   4.6 g
Cholesterol   1 mg
Sodium   < 125 mg

Ingredients

1 tsp extra-virgin olive oil, or as needed
1/2 yellow onion, diced
1 leek, diced
3 cloves garlic, minced
1 head cauliflower, cut into florets
1/2 head broccoli, cut into florets
3 red potatoes, cut into bite-size pieces
1 (32 oz.) carton low-sodium vegetable broth
water to cover

1 tbsp nutritional yeast, or more to taste
1/2 tsp ground turmeric
1 bay leaf
salt and ground black pepper to taste
1 pinch cayenne pepper, or to taste
1 (12 fluid oz.) can fat-free evaporated milk
3 tbsps whole wheat flour, or as needed
1 tbsp curry powder

Directions

1. Stir fry your garlic, leeks, and onions in olive oil, in a large pot, for 6 mins.
2. Then add: potatoes, cauliflower, and broccoli.
3. Cook everything for 6 more mins.
4. Now pour in your broth and increase the heat.
5. Add some water as well to submerge all the veggies.
6. Season everything with: black pepper, curry, cayenne, turmeric, salt, and bay leaves then place a lid on the pot, ajar, and let the contents simmer for 27 mins.
7. Get a bowl, combine: flour, yeast, and milk. Then pour everything into the soup.
8. Let the soup simmer for 6 more mins.
9. Enjoy.

Cream
of Cauliflower Bake

🥄 Prep Time: 40 mins
🕐 Total Time: 1 hr 10 mins

Servings per Recipe: 7
Calories	545 kcal
Fat	38.8 g
Carbohydrates	30g
Protein	20.5 g
Cholesterol	101 mg
Sodium	1544 mg

Ingredients

1/2 C. uncooked white rice
10 oz. broccoli florets
10 oz. cauliflower florets
1/2 C. butter
1 onion, diced
1 lb processed cheese food, cubed
1 (10.75 oz.) can condensed cream of

chicken soup
5 3/8 fluid oz. milk
1 1/2 C. crushed buttery round crackers

Directions

1. Set your oven to 350 degrees before doing anything else.
2. Begin to boil water in a large pot.
3. Once everything is boiling pour in your rice.
4. Get the water boiling again and the place a lid on the pot.
5. Set the heat to a low level and cook the rice for 22 mins with a gentle boil.
6. Once the rice is done begin to stir fry your onions in butter for 3 mins then add in your: cooked rice, cauliflower, and broccoli.
7. Toss the veggies in the butter and add the milk, soup, and cheese.
8. Cook everything until the cheese has melted and pour the contents into a casserole dish.
9. Top the casserole with crackers and cook everything in the oven for 32 mins.
10. Let the contents sit for 10 mins then serve.
11. Enjoy.

CAULIFLOWER
Salad I

Prep Time: 10 mins
Total Time: 25 mins

Servings per Recipe: 8
Calories	400 kcal
Fat	33 g
Carbohydrates	15.5g
Protein	11.2 g
Cholesterol	177 mg
Sodium	453 mg

Ingredients

1 C. broccoli florets
1 C. cauliflower florets
2 C. hard-cooked eggs, diced (optional)
1 C. shredded Cheddar cheese
6 slices bacon

1 C. mayonnaise
1/2 C. white sugar
2 tbsps white wine vinegar

Directions

1. Fry your bacon then remove any excess oils and break it into pieces.
2. Get a big bowl and layer: cauliflower, bacon, eggs, broccoli, and cheese.
3. Get a 2nd bowl, mix: vinegar, mayo, and sugar.
4. Pour the wet mix over the layers and chill everything in the fridge for 10 mins before serving.
5. Enjoy.

Beef
& Broccoli

Prep Time: 15 mins
Total Time: 6 hrs 45 mins

Servings per Recipe: 4
Calories	814 kcal
Fat	16 g
Carbohydrates	121.4g
Protein	46.4 g
Cholesterol	74 mg
Sodium	2167 mg

Ingredients

1 beef bouillon cube
1 C. warm water
1/2 C. soy sauce
1/3 C. brown sugar
2 cloves garlic, minced
1 tbsp sesame oil
1 1/2 lbs beef sirloin, cut into 1-inch strips

2 tbsps cornstarch
2 lbs broccoli florets, or to taste
2 C. cooked jasmine rice
1 tbsp sesame seeds, for garnish (optional)

Directions

1. Get a bowl, evenly mix: garlic, sesame oil, beef cubes, brown sugar, and warm water. Make sure everything dissolves nicely.
2. Cook on low for 8 hrs your beef strips and the sesame oil mix in the slow cooker.
3. Get a 2nd bowl, stir evenly: cornstarch and two tbsps of liquid from the crock pot. Add this back to the beef and stir nicely.
4. Cook for 35 more mins.
5. The broccoli is best cooked with a steamer insert inside of a saucepan for 7 mins, but can be cooked in the microwave as well.
6. Once the broccoli is cooked coat it with some sauce from the slow cooker.
7. Enjoy with jasmine rice.

BROCCOLI
Pepper Cheddar Grilled Cheese

 Prep Time: 10 mins

Total Time: 15 mins

Servings per Recipe: 1

Calories	689 kcal
Fat	55.2 g
Carbohydrates	30.6g
Protein	19.7 g
Cholesterol	151 mg
Sodium	950 mg

Ingredients

2 slices bread
2 slices Cheddar cheese
1/4 C. chopped broccoli
1/4 C. chopped zucchini
1/4 C. chopped green bell pepper

1 tbsp chopped jalapeno pepper
3 tbsps butter

Directions

1. Get a frying pan hot with nonstick spray.
2. Layer the following on a piece of bread: 1 piece of cheddar, bell pepper, broccoli, jalapeno, 1 piece of cheddar, and zucchini.
3. Top with remaining piece of bread. Coat the outside of the sandwich with butter.
4. Cook for 1 min per side in the frying pan, covered.
5. Enjoy.

Garden Lasagna I (Broccoli, Carrots, & Corn)

Prep Time: 30 mins
Total Time: 1 hr 10 mins

Servings per Recipe: 10
Calories   534 kcal
Carbohydrates   48.8 g
Cholesterol   103 mg
Fat   27 g
Protein   26.6 g
Sodium   1091 mg

Ingredients

1 box lasagna noodles
2 eggs, beaten
1 box part-skim ricotta cheese
2 cans condensed cream of mushroom soup
2 C. shredded Cheddar cheese
1 C. grated Parmesan cheese

1 C. sour cream
1 package herb and garlic soup mix
1 bag chopped frozen broccoli, thawed
1 bag frozen sliced carrots
1 bag frozen corn kernels

Directions

1. Set your oven to 375 degrees before anything else.
2. Boil noodles in water with salt for 10 mins. Remove all water, set aside.
3. Get a bowl, mix: soup mix, beaten eggs, sour cream, ricotta, parmesan, cheddar, and mushroom soup.
4. In your baking layer everything in the following manner: lasagna, cheese mix, carrots, corn, broccoli. Continue until all ingredients used. Cheese should be upmost layer.
5. Cook for 30, with a cover of foil. 10 mins without.
6. Enjoy.

PEPPERONI
Rotini Pasta Salad

 Prep Time: 15 mins
Total Time: 2 hrs 25 mins

Servings per Recipe: 8

Calories	415 kcal
Carbohydrates	25.6 g
Cholesterol	33 mg
Fat	29.1 g
Protein	13.9 g
Sodium	1518 mg

Ingredients

1 (16 ounce) package tri-color rotini pasta
1/4 pound sliced pepperoni sausage
1 cup fresh broccoli florets
1 (6 ounce) can black olives, drained and sliced

1 (8 ounce) package mozzarella cheese, shredded
1 (16 ounce) bottle Italian-style salad dressing

Directions

1. Cook pasta in salty boiling water for about 10 minutes until tender before draining it.

2. Mix pasta, dressing, pepperoni, cheese, broccoli and olives very thoroughly before refrigerating for at least an hour.

3. Serve.

Linguine
Romano Pasta Salad

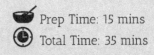 Prep Time: 15 mins

Total Time: 35 mins

Servings per Recipe: 6

Calories	275 kcal
Carbohydrates	32.2 g
Cholesterol	10 mg
Fat	12.8 g
Protein	9.9 g
Sodium	141 mg

Ingredients

1 (8 ounce) package linguine pasta
1 (12 ounce) bag broccoli florets, cut into bite-size pieces
1/4 cup olive oil
4 tsps minced garlic
1/2 tsp red pepper flakes
1/2 cup finely shredded Romano cheese

2 tbsps finely chopped fresh flat-leaf parsley
1/4 tsp ground black pepper
salt to taste

Directions

1. Cook linguine in salty boiling water for about 10 minutes until tender before draining it.
2. Steam broccoli for about 5 minutes with the help of steamer insert in a saucepan.
3. Cook garlic and red pepper flakes in hot oil for about 3 minutes before adding this and broccoli to the pot containing linguine.
4. Stir in Romano cheese, salt, parsley and black pepper.
5. Combine thoroughly before serving.

RAVIOLI
& Broccoli Pasta Salad

Prep Time: 15 mins
Total Time: 30 mins

Servings per Recipe: 4
Calories   653 kcal
Carbohydrates   66.9 g
Cholesterol   63 mg
Fat   31.7 g
Protein   28 g
Sodium   902 mg

Ingredients

2 (9 ounce) packages Refrigerated
Cheese Ravioli, cooked, chilled
1/4 cup extra virgin olive oil
4 large cloves garlic, finely chopped
1/4 cup red wine vinegar
2 medium tomatoes, chopped

2 cups broccoli florets
1 large green bell pepper, chopped
1/2 cup pitted and halved ripe olives
1/2 cup Refrigerated Parmesan
1/4 cup Refrigerated Romano Cheese

Directions

1. Cook garlic in hot oil for about one minute before mixing it with vinegar in a bowl.
2. Stir in tomatoes, Parmesan cheese, broccoli, bell pepper, olives, and Romano cheese before refrigerating it for at least an hour.

Mac
and Cheese Soup

Prep Time: 15 mins
Total Time: 30 mins

Servings per Recipe: 6
Calories	422 kcal
Carbohydrates	55.7 g
Cholesterol	42 mg
Fat	12.9 g
Protein	20.9 g
Sodium	1248 mg

Ingredients

1 (14 ounce) package uncooked macaroni and cheese
1 cup chopped broccoli
1/2 cup chopped onion
1 cup water
2 1/2 cups milk
1 (11 ounce) can condensed cream of

Cheddar cheese soup
1 cup cubed cooked turkey ham

Directions

1. Cook elbow macaroni in boiling salty water for about 8 minutes before draining it with the help of a colander.

2. Bring the mixture of broccoli, water and onion to boil, and cook until you see that broccoli is tender.

3. Now add macaroni, ham, cheese mixture, soup and milk into it before bringing all this to boil again.

4. Serve.

CHEESY
Onion and Potato Soup

 Prep Time: 15 mins
Total Time: 1 hr

Servings per Recipe: 6

Calories	183 kcal
Fat	8.1 g
Carbohydrates	21.7g
Protein	8.2 g
Cholesterol	14 mg
Sodium	297 mg

Ingredients

1 onion, diced
1 tbsp olive oil
2 heads broccoli, chopped
2 potatoes, peeled and cubed

4 C. chicken broth
4 oz. stilton cheese

Directions

1. Stir fry your onions in olive oil until see-through. Then add in your potatoes and broccoli and cook for 6 mins. Then add the broth and get the contents boiling. Once the broth is boiling set the heat to a lower level and let everything lightly boil for 23 mins with no cover.
2. Add the cheese after shutting the heat and let it melt. Use an immersion blender or regular food processor to blend the soup down to become smoother.
3. Then reheat it before serving.
4. Enjoy.

Cream
of Mushrooms and Broccoli

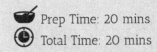 Prep Time: 20 mins

Total Time: 20 mins

Servings per Recipe: 4

Calories	645 kcal
Fat	42.7 g
Carbohydrates	39.7g
Protein	28.3 g
Cholesterol	151 mg
Sodium	355 mg

Ingredients

1/2 (16 oz.) package linguine
1 C. fresh or frozen broccoli flowerets
2 tbsps butter
1 lb skinless, boneless chicken breast, cut into cubes
1 (10.75 oz.) can cream of mushroom soup
1/2 C. milk

1/2 C. grated Parmesan cheese
1/4 tsp ground black pepper

Directions

1. Boil your pasta in water and salt for 5 mins then add in the broccoli and cook the mix for 5 more mins.
2. Now remove all the liquids.
3. Begin to stir fry your chicken in butter then once the meat is browned and done add: the pasta mix, cream of mushroom, black pepper, milk, and cheese.
4. Add a topping of parmesan and serve.
5. Enjoy.

2 CHEESE
Chicken Casserole

Prep Time: 20 mins
Total Time: 40 mins

Servings per Recipe: 8
Calories   580 kcal
Fat   28.6 g
Carbohydrates   30.1g
Protein   49.4 g
Cholesterol   164 mg
Sodium   453 mg

Ingredients

6 oz. egg noodles
3 tbsps butter
1 yellow onion, chopped
1/4 C. all-purpose flour
1 1/2 C. chicken broth
3/4 C. milk
salt and pepper to taste
5 C. cooked, shredded chicken breast meat

1 (10 oz.) package chopped frozen broccoli, thawed
1 C. shredded Cheddar cheese
1 C. shredded provolone cheese

Directions

1. Boil your pasta in water and salt for 9 mins. Then remove all the liquids.
2. Coat a baking dish with oil then set your oven to 400 degrees before doing anything else.
3. Now begin to stir fry your onions in butter for 4 mins then add in the flour.
4. Stir the contents then pour in the broth.
5. Stir the contents again until everything is smooth then begin to gradually add in your milk while continuing to stir.
6. Once the mix becomes thick with a medium level of heat add some pepper and salt.
7. Layer your pasta in your baking dish then place the chicken on top.
8. Add the broccoli over the chicken and coat everything with the broth mix.
9. Mix your cheese together then add 1/2 of the mix over the broccoli.
10. Cook the layers in the oven for 25 mins then add the rest of the cheese and let the casserole stand for 10 mins inside the oven with no heat.
11. Enjoy.

Swiss Style
Broccoli Casserole

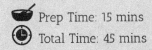 Prep Time: 15 mins

Total Time: 45 mins

Servings per Recipe: 8
Calories	441 kcal
Fat	33 g
Carbohydrates	15g
Protein	23.3 g
Cholesterol	148 mg
Sodium	285 mg

Ingredients

8 C. fresh broccoli
1/2 C. butter
2 tbsps all-purpose flour
1 small onion, chopped
1 1/4 C. milk

salt and pepper to taste
4 C. shredded Swiss cheese
2 eggs, beaten

Directions

1. Set your oven to 325 degrees before doing anything else.
2. Steam your broccoli over 2 inches of boiling water, with a steamer insert, for 5 mins. Then remove all the liquids.
3. Now being to stir and heat your flour and butter in a large pot. Continue stirring and heating until the mix is bubbling then add the onions and milk.
4. Get everything boiling and let it go for 60 secs.
5. Now shut the heat and add in some pepper and salt.
6. Combine in the eggs and cheese and add in the broccoli.
7. Stir the mix again then place everything into a baking dish.
8. Cook the broccoli for 40 mins in the oven.
9. Enjoy.

SWEET POTATO
Wraps

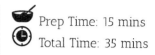 Prep Time: 15 mins
Total Time: 35 mins

Servings per Recipe: 6

Calories	356 kcal
Carbohydrates	65.2 g
Cholesterol	0 mg
Fat	5.6 g
Protein	11.4 g
Sodium	888 mg

Ingredients

2 sweet potatoes, peeled and cut into bite-size pieces
2 tbsps extra virgin olive oil
one cup broccoli florets
one (15 ounce) can lentils, drained and rinsed
one tbsp cumin
one 1/2 tsps cayenne pepper, or (your preferred amount)

one tsp garlic salt
2 tomatoes, chopped
6 tbsps barbeque sauce, divided
6 whole wheat Lebanese-style pita bread rounds

Directions

1. Let's begin this recipe by grabbing a cooking pot and filling it with water.
2. Combine the sweet potatoes with the water and heat everything over a high level of heat. Once the water has reached a boiling state lower the heating source to a medium to low level. Let the potatoes simmer for eight mins or until you find them soft.
3. Once the potatoes are soft remove them from the water. Grab a frying pan for the next step.
4. Place the frying pan over a medium to high level of heat and add some olive oil.
5. Let the olive oil get hot and add your broccoli. Take care to continually stir the contents until you find your veggies are soft but firm. This should take about 5 mins of frying.
6. Grab lentils and the following items: sweet potatoes, cayenne pepper, salt, and cumin. Combine all the items with the broccoli and fry for five mins.
7. Once all the contents have been nicely heated combine the diced tomatoes and continue cooking for an additional three mins.
8. Now get your pita ready by adding one tbsp of barbeque sauce to it.
9. Take a cup of potatoes & lentil mixture and place it on the pita for wrapping.

10. If you need some help keeping your pita secured take care to fold up the bottom portion first and then the sides. Use a toothpick hold it all together.

11. Plate and serve.

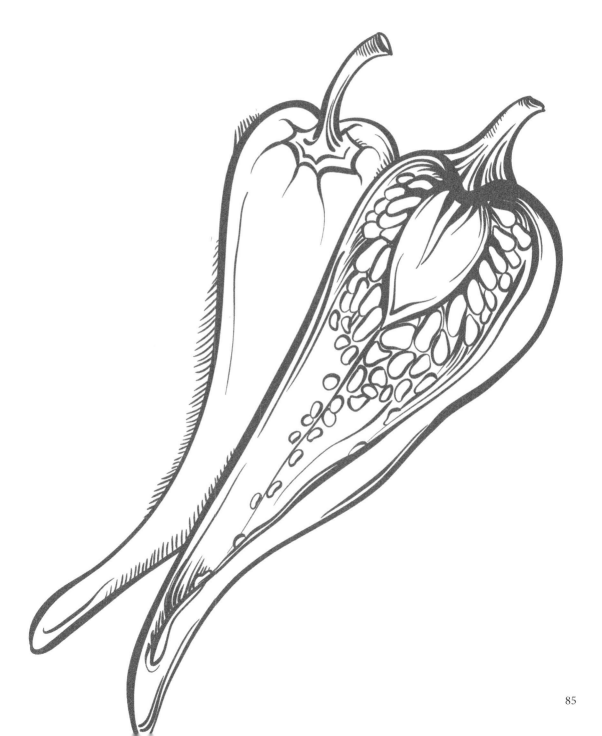

A QUICHE
of Lentils and Cheese

Prep Time: 15 mins
Total Time: 1 hr 30 mins

Servings per Recipe: 8

Calories	165 kcal
Fat	9.1 g
Carbohydrates	12.4g
Protein	9.7 g
Cholesterol	103 mg
Sodium	392 mg

Ingredients

1 C. diced onion
2 tbsps olive oil
1/2 C. dried lentils
2 C. water
2 C. broccoli florets
1 C. diced fresh tomatoes
4 eggs, beaten
1 C. milk

1 tsp salt
ground black pepper to taste
2 tsps Italian seasoning
1/2 C. shredded Cheddar cheese
(optional)

Directions

1. Set your oven to 375 degrees before doing anything else.
2. Combine some olive oil and onions in a pie plate and cook the mix in the oven for 17 mins.
3. At the same time get your lentils boiling in water and then cook them for 22 mins.
4. Now remove any leftover liquids.
5. Add the broccoli to the same pot as the lentils and place a lid over everything.
6. Cook this mix for 7 mins.
7. Combine the lentil mix and the tomatoes with the onions in the pie dish and then add the cheese as well.
8. Get a bowl, combine: Italian seasoning, eggs, pepper, salt, and milk.
9. Combine this mix with the lentils in the pie dish and cook everything in the oven for 50 mins.
10. Enjoy.

Swiss Style
Broccoli Casserole

Prep Time: 15 mins
Total Time: 45 mins

Servings per Recipe: 8
Calories   441 kcal
Fat   33 g
Carbohydrates   15g
Protein   23.3 g
Cholesterol   148 mg
Sodium   285 mg

Ingredients

8 C. fresh broccoli
1/2 C. butter
2 tbsps all-purpose flour
1 small onion, chopped
1 1/4 C. milk

salt and pepper to taste
4 C. shredded Swiss cheese
2 eggs, beaten

Directions

1. Set your oven to 325 degrees before doing anything else.
2. Steam your broccoli over 2 inches of boiling water, with a steamer insert, for 5 mins. Then remove all the liquids.
3. Now being to stir and heat your flour and butter in a large pot. Continue stirring and heating until the mix is bubbling then add the onions and milk.
4. Get everything boiling and let it go for 60 secs.
5. Now shut the heat and add in some pepper and salt.
6. Combine in the eggs and cheese and add in the broccoli.
7. Stir the mix again then place everything into a baking dish.
8. Cook the broccoli for 40 mins in the oven.
9. Enjoy.

CLASSIC
Chicken and Rice

🥘 Prep Time: 30 mins
🕐 Total Time: 1 hr 20 mins

Servings per Recipe: 6	
Calories	700 kcal
Fat	12.1 g
Carbohydrates	76.7g
Protein	67.7 g
Cholesterol	1161 mg
Sodium	1790 mg

Ingredients

2 C. white rice
4 C. water
2/3 C. soy sauce
1/4 C. brown sugar
1 tbsp cornstarch
1 tbsp minced fresh ginger
1 tbsp minced garlic
1/4 tsp red pepper flakes
3 skinless, boneless chicken breast
halves, thinly sliced
1 tbsp sesame oil

1 green bell pepper, cut into matchsticks
1 (8 oz.) can sliced water chestnuts, drained
1 head broccoli, broken into florets
1 C. sliced carrots
1 onion, cut into large chunks
1 tbsp sesame oil

Directions

1. In a pan, add the water and rice and bring to a boil on high heat.
2. Reduce the heat to medium-low and simmer, covered for about 20-25 minutes.
3. In a small bowl, add the brown sugar, corn starch and soy sauce and mix till a smooth mixture forms.
4. Add the garlic, ginger and red pepper flakes and mix well.
5. Add the chicken slices and coat everything with the mixture generously.
6. Cover and refrigerate to marinate for about 15-20 minutes.
7. In a large skillet, heat 1 tbsp of the oil on medium-high heat and stir fry the vegetables for about 5 minutes.
8. Transfer the vegetables onto a large plate and cover with some foil to keep them warm.
9. In the same skillet, heat the remaining oil on medium-high heat.
10. Remove the chicken slices from the refrigerator and place the chicken into the skillet, reserving the marinade.

11. Stir fry the chicken for about 2 minutes per side.
12. Add the reserved marinade and the vegetables mixture and bring to a boil.
13. Cook, stirring occasionally for about 5-7 minutes.
14. Serve the chicken mixture over the rice.

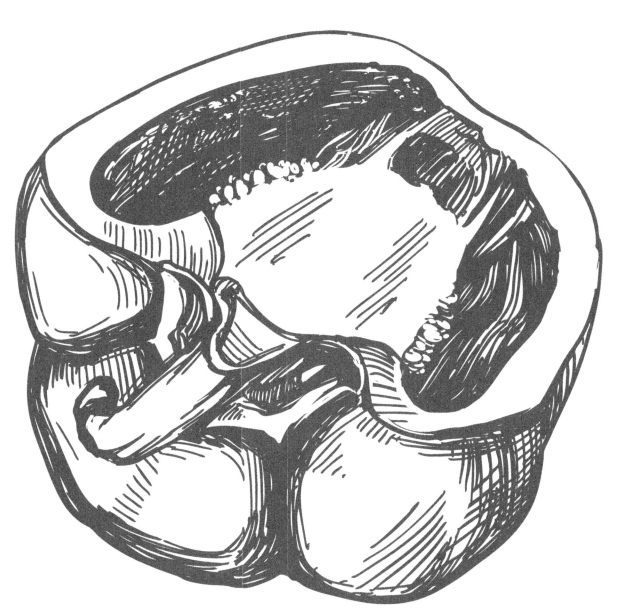

BROCCOLI
and Cheddar Quinoa

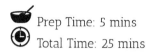

Prep Time: 5 mins
Total Time: 25 mins

Servings per Recipe: 4

Calories	299 kcal
Fat	12.3 g
Carbohydrates	32.9 g
Protein	14.8 g
Cholesterol	30 mg
Sodium	491 mg

Ingredients

2 C. chopped broccoli
1 3/4 C. vegetable broth
1 C. quinoa
1 C. shredded Cheddar cheese

salt and ground black pepper to taste

Directions

1. Boil, in a big pot: quinoa, broccoli, and broth.
2. Once boiling place a lid on the pot and lower the heat.
3. Let the quinoa gently boil for 17 mins. Then add your cheese.
4. Cook everything for 4 more mins until the cheese is melted and then add your preferred amount of pepper and salt.
5. Enjoy.

Southeast Asian
Tofu with Broccoli

Prep Time: 10 mins
Total Time: 20 mins

Servings per Recipe: 4
Calories	443 kcal
Fat	29.9 g
Carbohydrates	24g
Protein	29 g
Cholesterol	0 mg
Sodium	641 mg

Ingredients

1 tbsp peanut oil
1 small head broccoli, chopped
1 small red bell pepper, chopped
5 fresh mushrooms, sliced
1 lb firm tofu, cubed
1/2 C. peanut butter
1/2 C. hot water

2 tbsps vinegar
2 tbsps soy sauce
1 1/2 tbsps molasses
ground cayenne pepper to taste

Directions

1. Get a bowl, mix the following, until smooth: cayenne, peanut butter, molasses, hot water, soy sauce, and vinegar.
2. Stir fry your tofu, broccoli, mushrooms, and bell peppers in the oil for 7 mins.
3. Add in the peanut mix and cook for 6 more mins with a gentle boil.
4. Enjoy.

THAI
Stir-Fry Noodle

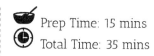 Prep Time: 15 mins

Total Time: 35 mins

Servings per Recipe: 3

Calories	758 kcal
Fat	9.9 g
Carbohydrates	140.1g
Protein	24.8 g
Cholesterol	99 mg
Sodium	1353 mg

Ingredients

1 tbsp dark soy sauce
2 tbsps soy sauce
1 tbsp white sugar, or more to taste
1 tsp Sriracha
1 tbsp olive oil
1 tbsp chopped garlic
6 oz. chicken tenders, cut into bite-size pieces

1 (16 oz.) package frozen broccoli
1 lb fresh flat rice noodles
1 egg, beaten
1/4 tsp sesame seeds
1 pinch crushed red pepper flakes

Directions

1. Get the following simmering in a saucepan: Sriracha, dark soy sauce, sugar, and regular soy sauce.
2. Let the mix simmer while stirring for 7 mins. Then shut the heat.
3. Now begin to stir fry your chicken and garlic in olive oil for 9 mins then add in the broccoli.
4. Let the mix continue to fry until the broccoli is done then add in your noodles and stir everything.
5. Top the mix with the sauce and stir everything again while heating the mix. Let everything get thick.
6. Make some space in your skillet then fry your egg in the space.
7. Scramble it as it cooks then mix everything together.
8. Top the dish with some pepper flakes and sesame seeds.
9. Enjoy.

Red Pepper Broccoli

 Prep Time: 5 mins

Total Time: 10 mins

Servings per Recipe: 5

Calories	61 kcal
Fat	3.8 g
Carbohydrates	5.6g
Protein	3.2 g
Cholesterol	0 mg
Sodium	27 mg

Ingredients

1 (16 oz.) package frozen broccoli, thawed, cleaned, dried
1 tbsp olive oil

1/2 tsp crushed red pepper flakes
salt, to taste

Directions

1. Add your pepper flakes to your olive oil and let the mix cook for 60 secs then add in the broccoli and let it cook for 6 mins.
2. After the broccoli has cooked add your salt then serve.
3. Enjoy.

BASIL
Broccoli

Prep Time: 10 mins
Total Time: 30 mins

Servings per Recipe: 6
Calories   608 kcal
Fat   29.4 g
Carbohydrates   74.2g
Protein   16.1 g
Cholesterol   14 mg
Sodium   191 mg

Ingredients

8 tbsps olive oil
2 tbsps butter
4 cloves garlic, minced
1 lb fresh broccoli florets
1 C. vegetable broth
1 C. chopped fresh basil

1 lb rigatoni pasta
2 tbsps grated Parmesan cheese

Directions

1. Boil your pasta in water and salt for 9 mins then remove all the liquids.
2. Now heat and stir your butter and oil.
3. Once the mix is hot begin to stir fry your broccoli and garlic for 4 mins then pour in the broth and get everything boiling.
4. Once the mix is boiling, place a lid on the pot, set the heat to low, and let the contents cook until the broccoli is soft.
5. Top the dish with the parmesan and serve.
6. Enjoy.

Broccoli
Stir Fry

 Prep Time: 15 mins

⏱ Total Time: 25 mins

Servings per Recipe: 4

Calories	81 kcal
Fat	5.6 g
Carbohydrates	6.2g
Protein	3.2 g
Cholesterol	2 mg
Sodium	< 144 mg

Ingredients

1 lb broccoli florets
3 tbsps finely grated Parmesan cheese
1 tsp brown sugar
2 tbsps olive oil
1 tsp red pepper flakes

1/4 tsp kosher salt
1/8 tsp freshly ground black pepper

Directions

1. Blanch your broccoli in boiling water for 60 seconds then immediately enter the veggies into some ice water.
2. Now lay the broccoli on some paper towel to drain it completely.
3. Get a bowl, combine: brown sugar and parmesan.
4. Now get your oil hot then begin to stir fry the broccoli for a few secs then add in the black pepper, salt, and pepper flakes.
5. Stir the broccoli then let everything cook for 3 mins.
6. Shut the heat and top the veggie with the parmesan mix.
7. Enjoy.

ZUCCHINI
and Carrots Quesadilla

Prep Time: 10 mins
Total Time: 40 mins

Servings per Recipe: 2
Calories	787 kcal
Fat	30.1 g
Carbohydrates	99.7g
Protein	33.1 g
Cholesterol	55 mg
Sodium	1309 mg

Ingredients

1 zucchini, cubed
1 head fresh broccoli, diced
1 red bell pepper, diced
1 carrot, diced
1 yellow onion, diced
4 small button mushrooms, diced

4 (10 inch) flour tortillas
1/2 C. shredded sharp Cheddar cheese
1/2 C. shredded Monterey Jack cheese

Directions

1. Line a baking dish or sheet with foil. Then turn on your broiler to its low setting if possible before doing anything else.
2. For 8 mins with a steamer cook the following over one inch of boiling water and covered: mushrooms, zucchini, onions, broccoli, carrots, and bell peppers.
3. Get your baking sheet or dish and put into it two tortillas. Layer the following: Monterey, vegetables, cheddar, and another tortilla.
4. Broil the contents until the cheese is bubbly. You should try to flip the tortillas to brown both sides, but this not necessary.
5. Enjoy.

California
Tortellini Soup

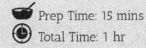 Prep Time: 15 mins

Total Time: 1 hr

Servings per Recipe: 8

Calories	176 kcal
Fat	4.9 g
Carbohydrates	20g
Protein	13.2 g
Cholesterol	36 mg
Sodium	1156 mg

Ingredients

1 (48 fluid oz.) can chicken broth
3 C. water
2 frozen skinless, boneless chicken breast halves - diced
1 small onion, diced
1 C. thinly sliced carrots
1 tsp lemon pepper

1 tsp dried oregano
1 dash garlic salt
2 C. fresh broccoli florets
1 (9 oz.) package frozen cheese tortellini
1/4 C. grated Parmesan cheese

Directions

1. Get your water and broth boiling.
2. Once the mix is boiling add in carrots, onions, chicken, garlic salt, lemon pepper, and oregano.
3. Now set the heat to low and let the mix cook for 30 mins.
4. At this point the chicken should be fully done. Add in the broccoli and continue simmering the veggies for 12 mins before adding the pasta and cooking the mix for 12 more mins.
5. Garnish the dish with your parmesan and serve.
6. Enjoy.

HEALTHY
Enchiladas

Prep Time: 40 mins
Total Time: 1 hr 50 mins

Servings per Recipe: 12

Calories	390 kcal
Fat	23.9 g
Carbohydrates	35.9 g
Protein	10.8 g
Cholesterol	54 mg
Sodium	210 mg

Ingredients

1 head broccoli, cut into florets
8 oz. whole button mushrooms
3 small zucchini, chopped
2 C. chopped carrots
1/4 C. olive oil
salt and pepper to taste
3 C. water
1 C. milk
1/4 C. butter

1 (7.6 oz.) package instant mashed potato flakes
1 (12 oz.) package corn tortillas
3 C. enchilada sauce
8 oz. shredded Cheddar cheese

Directions

1. Set your oven to 425 degrees F before doing anything else.
2. In a large bowl, mix together the broccoli, mushrooms, zucchini, carrots, olive oil, salt and black pepper.
3. In a shallow baking dish, spread the vegetable mixture in a single layer and cook in the oven for about 30-40 minutes, stirring once in the middle way.
4. Remove the vegetables from the oven.
5. Now, set the oven to 350 degrees F.
6. In a large pan, add the water, milk and butter and bring to a boil.
7. Remove the pan from the heat and mix in the mashed potato flakes and keep aside for about 2 minutes.
8. With a fork, stir the mashed potatoes till smooth.
9. Stir in the roasted vegetables.
10. Heat a dry, nonstick skillet on medium heat and quickly heat each tortilla from both sides to make pliable.
11. Dip the tortillas in enchilada sauce.

12. Place about 1/4-1/3 C. of the potato-veggie mixture in the center of each tortilla and top with about 1-2 tbsp of the cheese.

13. Roll the tortillas and in a 13x9-inch baking dish, place them, seam-side down.

14. Place the extra sauce on the top and sprinkle with the remaining cheese.

15. Cook in the oven for about 20-30 minutes.

VEGGIE CURRY
Caribbean Style

Prep Time: 20 mins
Total Time: 50 mins

Servings per Recipe: 6
Calories	190 kcal
Fat	9.4 g
Carbohydrates	25.8g
Protein	2.7 g
Cholesterol	0 mg
Sodium	19 mg

Ingredients

1 tsp ground cumin
1/2 tsp ground turmeric
1/2 tsp curry powder
1/2 tsp ground allspice
1/4 C. olive oil
1 tbsp grated fresh ginger root
1 small onion, chopped
4 cloves garlic, minced
2 potatoes, cut into small cubes

1/2 C. chopped red bell pepper
1/2 C. chopped broccoli
1 C. chopped bok choy
1 plantains, peeled and broken into chunks
1 C. water
salt to taste

Directions

1. In a small bowl, mix together the cumin, turmeric, allspice and curry powder.
2. In a skillet, heat the olive oil on medium-low heat and sauté the ginger and cumin mixture for about 5 minutes.
3. Add the onion and garlic and sauté for about 1-2 minutes.
4. Stir in the potatoes and cook for about 1-2 minutes.
5. Add the red bell pepper, broccoli, bok choy, plantains and enough water to reach about half-full and simmer, covered for about 20-25 minutes.
6. Season with the salt and serve.

Filipino
Filling Soup

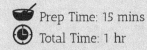 Prep Time: 15 mins

Total Time: 1 hr

Servings per Recipe: 6

Calories	304 kcal
Fat	19.7 g
Carbohydrates	15g
Protein	17.8 g
Cholesterol	51 mg
Sodium	1405 mg

Ingredients

2 tbsp canola oil
1 large onion, chopped
2 cloves garlic, chopped
1 lb. beef stew meat, cut into 1 inch cubes
1 quart water
2 large tomatoes, diced
1/2 lb. fresh green beans, rinsed and trimmed

1/2 medium head bok choy, cut into 1 1/2 inch strips
1 head fresh broccoli, cut into bite size pieces
1 (1.41 oz.) package tamarind soup base

Directions

1. In a pan, heat the oil and sauté the onion and garlic till tender.
2. Add the beef and seat till browned completely.
3. Add the water and bring to a boil.
4. Reduce the heat and simmer for about 20-30 minutes.
5. Add the tomatoes and green beans and simmer for about 10 minutes.
6. Stir in the bok choy, broccoli and tamarind soup mix and simmer for an about 10 minutes more.

NINGBO
Stir Fry

Prep Time: 30 mins
Total Time: 37 mins

Servings per Recipe: 6
Calories	74.8
Fat	4.8g
Cholesterol	0.0mg
Sodium	253.6mg
Carbohydrates	7.1g
Protein	2.5g

Ingredients

2 tbsp vegetable oil
1 medium onion, thinly sliced
1 tbsp freshly grated gingerroot
2 cloves garlic, minced
1/2 tsp salt
1/4 tsp red pepper flakes
3 C. sliced fresh broccoli florets

1 -1 1/2 lb bok choy, coarsely chopped
2 tbsp lemon juice
1 1/2 tsp sugar

Directions

1. In a large skillet, heat the oil on medium-high heat and sauté the onion, ginger, garlic, salt and red pepper flakes for about 2 minutes.

2. Add the broccoli and bok choy and stir-fry for about 1-2 minutes.

3. Add the lemon juice and sugar and stir-fry for about 3 minutes.

Printed in Great Britain
by Amazon

36146320R10057